HISTORY
OF THE
SEVENTY-THIRD INDIANA VOLUNTEERS
IN THE WAR OF 1861- 1865

Re-issued April 2009

James Keir Baughman

ISBN No. 978-0-9790443-6-6
James K. Baughman
www.baughmanliterary.com

ORIGINALLY COMPILED AND PUBLISHED BY A
COMMITTEE OF THE SEVENTY.THIRD
INDIANA REGIMENTAL ASSOCIATION
1909
THE CARNAHAN PRESS
Washington, D. C.

Copyright 2009, by the Publisher, James Keir Baughman.

All rights reserved.

No part of this Re-published Version may be reproduced or transmitted in any way, form, by any means, electronic or otherwise, including photocopying, recording, or by any information or retrieval system, or posted on the Internet or World Wide Web without the written permission of the Publisher, James Keir Baughman. This edition has been dramatically changed from the original and new copyright applies.

Re-published 2009 by James Keir Baughman, Fort Walton Beach, Florida. Significant contributions by Michael P. Downs, South Bend, IN, are gratefully acknowledged. Downs is a noted historian of the 73rd Indiana Volunteer Infantry Regiment. This volume is manufactured and printed in the United States.

www.baughmanliterary.com

ISBN # 978-0-9790443-6-6

Original Copyright 1909. This History was compiled and published by a Committee of the Seventy-third Indiana Regimental Association. First Edition manufactured and printed in the United States by The Carnahan Press, Washington, D.C.

Cover background art, the painting "Rock Of Erin" created by famed Civil War artist Don Troiani, is his depiction of the 69th Pennsylvania Volunteer Infantry defending against a wall of Confederates 12,000 men strong at the Battle of Gettysburg. As Artist and Publisher, Troiani's work may be found at Historical Art Prints. His web site address is www.historicalimagebank.com

TABLE OF CONTENTS

Preface

Prologue... Adj. Gen. Terrell's Sketch of Regiment

Chapter 1....From South Bend to Lexington, Ky

Chapter 2...From Louisville to Nashville

Chapter 3...From Nashville to Murfreesboro

Chapter 4....Streight's Raid.

Chapter 5....Annapolis to Indianapolis and Morgan's Raid

Chapter 6....Libby Prison

Chapter 7....History of Detachment with the 65th Ohio

Chapter 8....Return of Seventy-Third to Tennessee

Chapter 9... Battle of Athens, Ala

Chapter 10...Battle of Decatur, Ala

Chapter 11...Evacuate and Reoccupy North Alabama

Chapter 12...Fall of Richmond and End of War

Chapter 13...Roster, Regimental Field & Staff Officers

Chapter 14...Roster, Officers & Men of the Companies
Company A
Company B
Company C
Company D
Company E

Chapter 15...Roster, Officers & Men of the Companies
Company F
Company G
Company H
Company I
Company K

Chapter 16...Colonels of the Regiment

Chapter 17...History of the 73rd Regimental Association

Publication Committee of the 73rd Indiana Regimental Association...Leander P. Williams, Job Barnard, John M. Caulfield, Wilber E. Gorsuch, Ed A. Jernegan, and Henry C. Morgan, appointed during the years 1903 thru 1907.

PREFACE

The Committee charged with the preparation of this history fully appreciates its imperfections, but at the same time it realizes the difficulty of compiling a more accurate record at this late date, when so many of our number have passed away, and the memories of those who survive have become somewhat dim as to details.

We trust, however, that the following pages will preserve to the boys now living, and to the children and descendants of all, a substantially correct record of the services of the regiment.

We have taken the history prepared by Corporal Ezra Barnhill, from the diary of Colonel Wade, and which was published in the South Bend Tribune as the foundation for the present story of the regiment. This contained some apparent errors, which we have endeavored to correct from other documentary evidence. Among these documents is a diary kept by one of the Committee (Sergeant Barnard) during the time of his service.

We have not had, however, the benefit of any diary or journal kept continuously in the regiment, and have been obliged to fill in certain gaps from cotemporaneous letters, military reports, and other data, during the time when Colonel Wade and Sergeant Barnard were neither of them with it.

This Committee was appointed by the Seventy-third Regimental Association at its meeting held in Crown Point, Ind., in September, 1903. It then consisted of three members, namely, Wilbur E. Gorsuch, John N. Caulfield, and Henry C. Morgan.

Subsequently, Leander P. Williams was added to the Committee and, in 1907, Job Barnard was added. On the death of Henry C. Morgan, Edward A. Jernegan was named in his place.

That portion of this story which relates to the Streight raid, the prison life of the officers, and the escape from Libby Prison, was prepared by Lieutenant Williams, who was one of those who escaped through the tunnel, and returned safely to the Union lines.

Soon after the war Lieutenant Williams was made a Major by brevet, by the nomination of the President and confirmation by the Senate, and has since been generally called by that title. He has written this account of life in Libby from his own recollection and experiences, and memoranda made while there, and from other data published by his companions, but he wishes hereby to specially acknowledge his indebtedness to Lieutenant Alva C. Roach, of the Fifty-first Indiana, for his valuable publication, entitled, "A Prisoner of War."

PROLOGUE

Adj. Gen. Terrell's Sketch of the Regiment.

The Seventy-third Regiment was organized and mustered into service on the 16th of August, 1862, at South Bend, with Gilbert Hathaway as Colonel.

The regiment was recruited entirely from the Ninth Congressional district, and entered the service one thousand and ten strong, in less than three weeks from the date recruiting commenced.

It was ordered at once to Lexington, by way of Louisville, Kentucky. The defeat of the Union forces at Richmond, Kentucky, on the 30th of August, necessitated the evacuation of Lexington, and the regiment made a long and weary march to Louisville, distant ninety miles.

On the 1st of October, the Seventy-third was assigned to the Twentieth Brigade (Harker's) of the Sixth Division (Wood's) of Buell's army, commencing the pursuit of Bragg. On the 8th of October it was deployed in line in reserve and witnessed the battle of Chaplin Hills (or Perryville), losing one man killed.

It then pursued Bragg as far as Wild Cat, with slight skirmishing. Returning, it marched to Glasgow, Kentucky, and from thence to Gallatin, Tennessee, where, on the 7th of November, it surprised the enemy, driving him out of the place, and capturing nineteen prisoners.

On the 26th of November the regiment marched into Nashville, having previously encamped for several days at Silver Springs and engaged in an expedition to Lebanon.

While foraging, on the 1st and 25th of December, it skirmished with the enemy, and on the 26th of December marched with the army, under General Rosecrans, to engage the enemy. Pressing him back with skirmishing,

Harker's Brigade going to support Johnson on the morning of December 31, 1862. The Seventy-Third is on the right flank.

the army reached Stones River on the 29th, and on the evening of that day the Seventy-third, with the Fifty-first Indiana, was the first of the whole army to cross Stones River, under the fire of the enemy.

The Twentieth Brigade, encountering Breckenridge's whole division, was compelled to re-cross, which was effected after dark without serious loss.

On the 30th, the day was passed in artillery firing and sharp skirmishing.

On the 31st most terrific fighting occurred. The right wing of our army was driven back two miles, and the Twentieth Brigade was double-quicked a mile and a half to reinforce it, and, taking the position on the extreme right of the whole army, immediately engaged two rebel brigades.

The Seventy-third fought for twenty minutes at very close range, losing more than one-third of the number engaged, and then, charging, drove the force in its front from the field, and in turn was compelled to fall back a short distance by a rebel brigade on its flank.

But the enemy's advance was checked and the right wing and army saved by the desperate fighting made at this point.

General Rosecrans complimented the regiment in person immediately after the battle and recognized these facts. More or less fighting, with some loss to the regiment, occurred on the 1st and 2d of January, 1863.

During these operations the regiment was at the front and under fire for six days, and on the 3rd of January, being completely exhausted, it was placed in reserve. The enemy retreated the same day.

During this battle the regiment occupied, at different times, the following important positions: the extreme right of the whole army, the extreme left, and the centre. Every member of the color guard, except the color-bearer, was either killed or wounded. The regiment lost twenty-two killed, forty-six wounded, and thirty-six missing.

On the l0th of April the regiment was assigned to Colonel A. D. Streight's "Independent Provisional Brigade," organized and mounted for the purpose of penetrating into the enemy's country and cutting his communications.

Embarking at Nashville on steamers, it moved down the Cumberland and up the Tennessee River, disembarking at Eastport, Mississippi. The brigade was mounted by impressments from the country and moved by land to Tuscumbia, Alabama, in company with General Dodge's Division of the Sixteenth Army Corps.

On the 28th of April the "Independent Provisional Brigade" left Tuscumbia on its perilous expedition. General Dodge's division was to have cooperated by a movement eastward, but failed of success.

On the morning of the 30th of April, at Day's Gap, Alabama, the Provisional Brigade, numbering fifteen hundred, was attacked by four thousand cavalry, under. Generals Forrest and Roddy. The Seventy-third occupied the left flank of the line formed and gallantly repulsed a fierce charge made by the enemy, some of whom charged, within twenty feet of its colors. The whole brigade then charged the enemy's line and drove him from the field, capturing two fine pieces of artillery.

The brigade at once pushed southward to execute its mission, but the enemy, having collected his scattered cavalry, overtook and attacked the brigade late in the afternoon, at Crooked Creek, Alabama. A spirited engagement was kept up until night closed the battle, with a loss to the Seventy-third during the day of twenty-three killed and wounded. The enemy, however, was repulsed with a heavy loss.

On the 2nd of May the brigade was again attacked at Blount's Farm, Alabama. The Seventy-third bore the brunt of this fight. Here the gallant Colonel Gilbert Hathaway fell mortally wounded while at the head of, and cheering on, his men.

On the 3rd of May, Colonel Streight, being nearly out of ammunition and exhausted by five days' incessant traveling and skirmishing, and surrounded by superior forces, surrendered his brigade to the enemy at Cedar Bluffs., Alabama, on most honorable conditions, which, after surrender, were basely violated by the enemy.

The men were soon forwarded north and exchanged. The officers were kept in close confinement nearly two years, with the exception of a few who were specially exchanged or escaped.

The men of the regiment were kept in parole camp for several months, and then sent to Tennessee, where, on the 28th of March, 1864, Major Wade, being released from rebel prison, assumed the command of the regiment.

During the spring of 1864 the regiment was engaged in guarding the Nashville and Chattanooga Railroad, and during the summer it was placed on duty picketing the Tennessee River from Draper's Ferry to Limestone Point, with headquarters at Triana.

While performing this duty many encounters occurred between parties, of the enemy and detachments from the regiment, in nearly all of which success attended the Union arms.

For its bravery and efficiency in this line of duty the regiment was several times complimented by General Granger. During this time, and until April, 1865, the regiment was attached to the First Brigade, Fourth Division, Twentieth Army Corps.

In the latter part of September, 1864, the regiment, after having been engaged in defending Prospect, Tennessee, during Wheeler's raid, was ordered to Decatur, Alabama, and from thence to Athens, Alabama, which place Forrest had captured a few days before with a garrison of six hundred.

The enemy abandoning the place, Lieutenant-Colonel Wade was ordered to hold it, and at once put it in a condition for defense, constructing a bomb-proof in the fort, etc.

At three o'clock in the afternoon of the 1st of October the pickets of the Seventy-third were driven in by the enemy, who numbered four thousand cavalry and four pieces of artillery, under command of General Buford. The garrison numbered five hundred men and two pieces of artillery.

Skirmishing continued during the rest of the day.

At six o'clock next morning the enemy opened with a fierce artillery fire, which was kept up without intermission for two hours. The rebel firing was extremely accurate. Our artillery spiritedly replied, inflicting much loss on the enemy, while the bomb-proof, affording ample protection to our forces, no loss was sustained by the garrison.

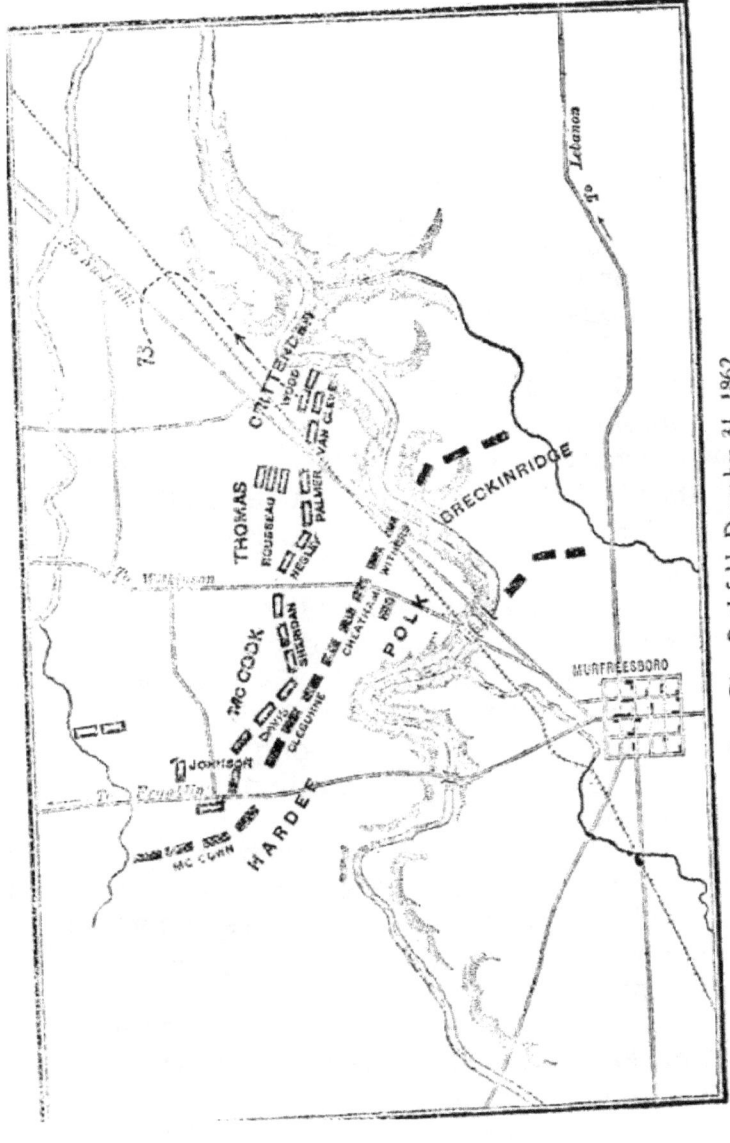

Stone River Battlefield, December 31, 1862.

The Seventy-Third lay in line of battle on that night, after an all day's fight, where the figures "73" are shown.

At eight o'clock a.m. General Buford sent in a flag of truce and demanded the surrender of the place, which was promptly refused.

As soon as the flag of truce disappeared the fire upon the enemy was resumed.

The enemy repulsed at every point, retired in haste

On the 26th of October, General Hood appeared before, and invested, Decatur, Alabama, with an army of thirty-five thousand men.

The Seventy-third had previously been ordered to that place to assist in its defense. The Union garrison numbered five thousand, and so stubborn was the resistance they made to the large army investing the place that after four days' fighting Hood raised the siege and withdrew his army, saying that "it would cost more to take the place than it was worth."

In the engagement the Seventy-third bore an honorable part, losing one killed and six wounded.

Part of the winter of 1864 was passed in Stevenson, Alabama, and in January, 1865, it was moved to Huntsville, and then placed on duty along the line of the Memphis and Charleston Railroad, with headquarters at Larkinsville, Alabama.

While upon this line skirmishing with the enemy was of almost daily occurrence. On the 16th of February, a detachment of twenty men repulsed an attacking party of rebel cavalry, killing and wounding five and taking one wounded prisoner.

On the 30th of April, fifteen men from Company D attacked thirty rebel cavalry, killing two and wounding two, without loss to themselves.

Other skirmishes occurred in which the regiment lost four killed and two wounded.

The regiment remained on this duty till the summer of 1865, when it proceeded to Nashville, where, on the 1st of July, 1865, it was mustered out of service.

Returning home, the Seventy-third was publicly

received in the State House grove at Indianapolis and addressed by Governor Morton and General Hovey.

The remaining recruits were transferred to the Twenty-ninth Indiana, with which regiment they still continue to serve, it being stationed at Marietta, Georgia, at the close of this sketch – November, 1865.

Chapter One

FROM SOUTH BEND TO LEXINGTON

On the 28th day of June, 1862, Governor Morton, of Indiana, and the governors of seventeen other states united in a communication to President Lincoln, urging him to call at once upon the several states for men sufficient to fill up the military organizations then in the field, and to add to the armies enough men to garrison and hold all the cities and positions which had then been captured, and to speedily crush the rebellion then still existing in several of the southern states.

In response to this patriotic appeal, and fully concurring in the wisdom of the views expressed by the Governors, the President, on July I, 1862, stated that he had decided to call into service an additional force of three hundred thousand men, and suggested that the troops should be chiefly of infantry.

On this call being made by the President, Governor Morton, on July 7th, 1862, issued his call for one regiment from each congressional district. In this call the Governor, after stating the honorable position which the State had occupied thus far in the contest, and the necessity for more men, said :

"I, therefore, call upon every man, whatever may be his rank and condition in life, to put aside his business and come to the rescue of his country. Upon every man, individually, let me urge the solemn truth, that whatever may be his condition or business, he has no duty or business half so important to himself and family as the speedy and effectual suppression of the rebellion."

Under this call the Governor directed that the Seventy-third Indiana Infantry should be raised in the Ninth

Congressional District, then represented by Hon. Schuyler Colfax, and that it should be located at South Bend.

A camp was accordingly established in the fair grounds and designated as "Camp Rose," to which all the men volunteering in that district were required to report.

The ten companies forming the Seventy-third Regiment were enlisted from only six of the fourteen counties then constituting the Ninth Congressional District, namely, Lake, Porter, LaPorte, St. Joseph, Marshall, and Cass.

The number of men volunteering in response to the Governor's call exceeded the number required to constitute one regiment, and another, the Eighty-seventh Indiana Infantry, with Kline G. Shryock, of Rochester, as Colonel, was organized during, and immediately following, the time of the organization of the Seventy-third, and in the same camp.

The Seventy-third was mustered in on the 16th of August, and the Eighty-seventh on the 31st of August.

The period of enlistment was prescribed in the call of the Governor to be for "three years, or during the war."

While in Camp Rose the regiment received a fine silk flag, presented by the patriotic ladies of South Bend, Mr. Colfax making the presentation speech on behalf of the donors. The ladies also furnished a dinner to all the Camp Rose soldiers, which was spread on long tables in the grove nearby, and was much appreciated by the boys.

Wednesday morning, August 20th, we went on board the train and started for the front. It was supposed at that time that we were only going to Indianapolis, but Louisville, Kentucky, was our destination. The boys had not yet received their guns, and only a portion of them had received uniforms.

After entering the train, Mr. Colfax, among many other leading citizens, appeared at the station to bid us good-bye and wish us all God-speed. He went along beside the train from car to car, stretching up to shake hands with all who were near enough to reach him.

As the train started from South Bend, the crowds that had gathered on each side bade the soldiers goodbye by waving flags, handkerchiefs and hats, and loudly cheering them on their way.

The regiment arrived at Jeffersonville next morning about nine o'clock, crossed the Ohio River on a steamboat to Louisville, and went into camp southwest of and near the city, where uniforms were issued to all who had not received them, and five large "Sibley" tents were drawn by each company, and "Harper's Ferry Muskets" were given us, with cartridge boxes and belts, and a supply of cartridges.

There was much objection on the part of some of the men to taking these muzzle-loading, smooth-bore guns because they had expected "Springfield" or "Enfield" rifles. However, the guns were taken, drilling began, and the boys soon became reasonably reconciled to the life of the soldier.

It was found subsequently that these guns, with ball and three buckshot, did good execution at short range when the regiment was engaged in battle.

On Sunday, August 24th, we received marching orders, broke camp, and marched to the station at Louisville and went on board a train of freight cars for Lexington, where we arrived about half-past six o'clock on Monday morning. We marched to a grove not far from the station and received a hearty breakfast furnished by the good people of Lexington, who brought in baskets of corn bread and other good things for the hungry boys.

In the afternoon a further march of about one mile was made, and a camp established in a fine grove near the road on premises belonging to the rebel general, John C. Breckenridge. After establishing a camp, we were daily instructed in company and regimental drill.

In this camp we first began to learn how to prepare

and police our quarters; how to cook and eat our rations; what reveille and roll-call meant, and sick-call, and guard-mount, and the final signal to put out lights at night. We sometimes obtained passes to go out of camp, and some will remember the peaches and melons which came into camp in some mysterious manner from the "Montague" place down the pike, or other farms in that neighborhood.

Here company tents and individual property, knapsacks, haversacks, etc., were marked for identification by amateur painters, with names, initials, letters and numbers.

On August 30th tents were struck, and we marched out about half a mile toward "Camp Dick Robinson," where we halted, faced about, and returned to our old camp.

In the evening of that day we were again called out, and started toward Richmond, Kentucky, where a battle was in progress, leaving Lieutenant Wolf, of Company F, with a detail of twenty men, in charge of the camp equipage and baggage in the old camp.

The night before, the first casualty occurred in the regiment, when Charles Kanarr, of Company I, being on guard, and carrying his gun in an awkward position, accidentally shot a charge through his right hand.

After making a night march of some twelve miles, we came within a short distance of the Kentucky River and met stragglers from the Union army on the retreat, and it transpired that the Union forces had been defeated by Kirby Smith, and were falling back.

The Seventy-third was then brigaded with the Fifty-second, Ninety-third and One hundred and fifth Ohio Infantry, the brigade being commanded by Colonel Anderson, of the Ninety-third Ohio.

We returned to Lexington Sunday night, August 31st, and reached our old camp a little after dark, and remained there until Monday night, when we were called out, with loaded guns, anticipating an attack, but no one appearing, we returned to camp, put on our knapsacks, loaded our wagons, and started for Louisville on a general retreat.

Reaching Versailles before morning, a halt was made of two hours, and then the march was resumed, the command reaching Frankfort Tuesday night, after a hard day's march, where we camped in a hollow.

Wednesday morning the march was resumed, and we camped that night on a hill, and the men all slept on their arms.

Thursday was another hard day's march, with a camp at night until about 1:30 o'clock on Friday morning, when the command again started for Louisville.

The regiment reached Louisville Friday evening, September 5, exhausted by the hard march and the heat. Water was scarce, and the air was full of lime dust along the pike, and the boys suffered severely. Some died on the way from sunstroke, and one Ohio soldier was thrown from a mule and killed. Several were taken prisoners by the Rebel Cavalry.

The Seventy-third, all being green troops, started from Lexington with knapsacks heavily laden, and had not yet learned how to travel light. Many blankets, knapsacks, and other impedimenta were thrown away on this march, and those who had come through safely and were still able for duty had learned their first lesson in the school of experience in a real forced march.

While the regiment was at Lexington, Adjutant Wade joined it, and after establishing a camp in Louisville, he began the preparation of regimental and company books and records. Private Job Barnard, of Company K, was detailed as his clerk, and assisted him in this Work.

Chapter Two

FROM LOUISVILLE TO NASHVILLE

On the march from Lexington, and sometime after reaching Louisville, our regiment was in the Division commanded by General James S. Jackson, and our Brigade Commander was General William T. Ward, of Kentucky.

As the army was then organized, ours was the First Brigade, First Division, of the Army of Kentucky, and after reaching Louisville was composed of the Ninety- third, Ninety-fourth and Ninety-eighth Ohio, and the Seventy-third Indiana. During the absence of General Ward, on account of illness, Colonel Hathaway was in command of the brigade for several days.

On September 16th we left camp with our knapsacks on and two days' rations in our haversacks, with five in the wagons, and with gun and accoutrements, marched into the city of Louisville and waited in the street for some time, when the order was given, "to the rear, open order, march," when we presented arms, and General Jackson and staff rode down the line. After being thus reviewed the regiment was formed in platoons and we marched through. the hot sun around the city and back to our old camp, where we pitched tents at the same place we occupied before. This review was severe on the boys. Many fell out and were not able to get back into camp. Some died from heat and fatigue.

Lieutenant John G. Greenawalt, of Company C, was detailed on General Ward's staff at this time as Acting Inspector, and later served as Acting Assistant Adjutant General of the Brigade, until July I, 1863, when he reported to the regiment at Indianapolis.

While in Louisville we had for the first time a sutler,

Mr. H. Humrichouser, from Plymouth, of whom we could buy small articles needed by us in our daily camp life.

On September 27th we learned that General Buell had arrived in Louisville and taken charge of the forces here.

Among the troops here from our own part of the state are the Ninth Indiana, Fifteenth Indiana, and the Eighty-seventh Indiana, the latter regiment being next us on our left. The Fourth Indiana Cavalry is in this vicinity also. Governor Morton visited our camp near Louisville one day and rode through our lines in company with General Garfield. We received him with loud cheers.

On the reorganization of the army after General Buell reached Louisville, we were put into what was called the Twentieth Brigade, Sixth Division, in the Army of the Ohio, the brigade being composed of the Fifty-first and Seventy-third Indiana, Sixty-fourth and Sixty-fifth Ohio, Thirteenth Michigan, and Sixth Ohio Battery, and our Division Commander was General Thomas J. Wood.

General James A. Garfield had commanded the brigade, but he, not being present, the brigade was then commanded by Colonel Charles G. Harker, of the Sixty-fifth Ohio.

On the 29th of September we were still in camp, and were engaged in throwing up fortifications in the cemetery.

September 30th the regiment moved camp in order to be with the rest of the brigade, and many of the boys seemed greatly relieved to be under a different division commander from that of General Jackson. He had the reputation of being tyrannical by reason of the hard march on the retreat from Lexington, and also by reason of the review in Louisville. But whether these criticisms among the private soldiers were well founded or not it may be difficult to determine at this time. He may have been obeying orders of those higher in authority and acting according to his best judgment, from right motives.

Whatever the fact may have been, the soldiers all respected him for his bravery, and when he was later killed at the battle of Perryville they were prompt to recognize in him true soldierly qualities.

On October 1st we started with the whole army, marching after General Bragg. We were in Crittenden's Corps, and marched forward on the central road toward Bardstown. The first day's march was eight miles, when we went into camp. The second night we camped near Salt River.

On the 4th of October we passed through Fairfield, and on the night of that day reached Bardstown. The enemy had just left a few hours before we reached there. The citizens seemed glad to welcome us in place of the rebels, who had been trading confederate scrip for the produce of the country and had told the citizens that they would make it good in Kentucky before spring.

The country around Bardstown was rough and cavernous, and suggested that Kentucky was the right place in which to locate the "Mammoth Cave."

We left Bardstown on the 5th of October, and marched in the direction of Harrodsburg, and camped that night at Beach Fork.

On the 6th broke camp at an early hour and made a rapid march of twelve miles in the hot sun and choking dust to Springfield. While on the way we passed a burning mill where the Eighty-seventh Indiana had been engaged in a lively skirmish with the rebels, killing two and putting the balance to flight. Camped at Springfield that night.

On the 7th marched again, halting for a short time in the afternoon, after which we started on and marched all night, getting into camp at dawn on October 8th. We remained in camp until the middle of the day, when orders came to move forward rapidly toward Perryville, where a battle was in progress. We formed in line of battle about five o'clock, and deployed skirmishers, and moved on through field and forest, hill and valley, until night, when we were within hearing of the battle, and where we slept on our arms, remaining in line of battle all night.

We expected to be called into action on the morning of the 9th, but learned that Bragg had retreated during the night and that our services in that capacity would not be needed.

We remained in camp and walked over the battlefield, where we saw many of the dead lying in ghastly rows, waiting burial. Portions of the field were strewn with guns which the rebels had thrown down and left. Some of our regiments were badly cut up in this engagement, General McCook's Corps doing the principal part of the fighting on behalf of our army.

In this battle our army lost two generals, Jackson and Terrill, and the Seventy-third lost one man, Charles Swinney, of Company K, who was detailed with the artillery.

On October 10th we left camp and marched a few miles through a cold rain.

October 11th we marched in line of battle most of the day over hills, through valleys, woods, brush and briers, leveling fences before us, and knocking down stone walls, until we reached Harrodsburg, from whence the enemy had just made its exit.

We went into camp and built up large fires, the air being chilly, and after dark we received orders to leave our fires burning and move out quietly, which we did, going something like a mile away from the camp, and lying down for the night without building fires. This move was made as a precaution for fear that we should be attacked in the night, our brigade alone being in advance and the enemy just having left, their main force being within a short distance from us, as we were informed by prisoners taken.

At this point a large hospital filled with rebel sick

and wounded fell into our hands.

On October 12th we marched on in pursuit of the enemy for some miles and then rejoined our division in the evening.

On the 13th we marched on, camping near the city of Danville, and our regiment was ordered out on picket duty. At midnight we received orders to return to camp from picket and immediately to break camp and proceed on the march, and we marched by moonlight through Danville and on toward Stanford.

On the 14th we heard cannonading in front, and halted a while in line of battle. We understood there was a force of rebel cavalry in our advance, which we overtook just before reaching Stanford. Passing through that town we camped near there for the night.

On the 15th we broke camp at an early hour and marched on through Crab Orchard, reaching that place about noon. This is a hilly region of the country in Rock Castle County. Our advance guard was skirmishing with the rear guard of the enemy most of the day.

On the 16th we marched out about half a mile and spent the day lying at rest in the road, and toward sundown we returned to the same camp we occupied the night before, and rested there on the 17th.

Resumed our march on the 18th and marched about ten miles through a very rough country, passing through Mount Vernon, the county seat of Rock Castle County, and camping about seven miles beyond. This became known as "Camp Starvation," as we were short of rations and the country was sparsely settled. We found walnuts, butter nuts and chestnuts, and a few of us strayed from the camp and obtained corn bread and other provisions at some of the remote farm houses.

On the 22nd we broke camp and returned to Crab Orchard and passed on through, camping about three miles beyond, making a march of some twenty-three miles on very scant rations.

On the 23d we passed on through Stanford, the county seat of Lincoln County, and through Hustinville, in Casey County, camping about four miles from the latter place.

Our division was now moving toward Columbia, and on the 24th we marched on through Liberty , the county seat of Casey County, and camped about ten miles beyond on the Green River.

On the 25th, reached Columbia and pitched tents. This was known as the snowy camp, as there was quite a heavy fall of snow for this country, although we were fairly well sheltered by our tents in the woods. The snow fell to the depth of about four inches. Several of the regiments in our division were destitute of tents, blankets, or overcoats, but the Seventy-third was fairly well provided with these.

We remained in this camp until the morning of the 30th, when we struck tents and resumed our march over rocky roads, reaching Edmonton at night, after a march of some twenty-three miles, and camped there near good water.

On the 31st we marched on to within five miles of Glasgow, where we found good water and plenty of black walnuts, marching this day only about thirteen miles. Near this camp we found plenty of good fence rails for fires.

On November 1st we struck tents at about five o'clock in the morning and marched on through Glasgow and camped a mile beyond at about 11 o'clock, making a march of some six miles, and found a very beautiful camp and pleasant weather.

We remained over Sunday and until the evening of November 4th, when we started on about dark, and after marching some five miles camped again for the rest of the night.

On the morning of the 5th we marched on to Scottsville, the county seat of Allen County, some twenty miles distant, where we remained in camp on the 6th.

Hiram S. Root, a private in Company K, died on the morning of the 5th shortly after we broke camp. Being sick and unable to march, he was left behind with some of his comrades, who stayed with him until he died, and they buried him and carved his initials on the bark of a beech tree standing near-by.

On November 7th we marched through a snow storm, and about 11 o'clock reached the state line and entered Sumner County, Tennessee.

On the 8th we left camp at 1:30 o'clock in the morning and marched to Gallatin, the county seat of Sumner County, by sunrise, a distance of fourteen miles, in pursuit of Morgan's cavalry. Found their camp freshly deserted. We took a few prisoners and cooked our breakfast over their camp fires, which were still left burning. We remained in camp until about noon, when we marched on the Lebanon road and camped on the banks of the Cumberland River, two or three miles from Gallatin.

On the 9th we remained in camp and rested, it being Sunday, and we had religious services, the Rev. J. M. Whitehead, chaplain of the Fifteenth Indiana, preaching to us.

We made a ten mile march on the 10th, across the Cumberland and out on the pike toward Nashville.

Camped at Silver Springs, where we remained until the 15th. On that day we marched to Lebanon and back again with our division in an effort to catch Morgan and his men. They escaped us, however.

On the 19th we marched on about seven miles nearer Nashville, and on the morning of the 20th marched a few miles further and fixed our camp at Spring Place, where we remained until the 26th. On that date, about 11 o'clock, we left camp and marched on to Nashville, going into camp near the railroad.

We remained in this camp and in this vicinity until after Christmas. There were a great number of troops in this immediate vicinity, and the bugles and drums were heard morning and evening, from reveille to tatoo, and the camp fires at night gave a picturesque scene.

On December 1st the regiment went out foraging and to guard a forage train. The guard consisted of the Seventy-third Indiana, five companies of the Thirteenth Michigan, and two pieces of artillery from the Sixth Ohio Battery, the whole guard commanded by Colonel Hathaway. We were to load and guard a train of sixty-five wagons, and it was a difficult task, but was accomplished without the loss of a man, although there was skirmishing during the day by artillery and musketry. The wagons were loaded at a mill on Mill Creek, across which the bridge had been burned.

On December 4th General Rosecrans, who was now commanding the army, had a grand review of the troops.

On December 8th our brigade went as guard for a forage train on the Nolinsville Pike. The only company engaged in skirmishing during the day was Company H.

On the 14th the Seventy-third went foraging again in company with a cavalry regiment, going out on the Lebanon Pike as far as The Hermitage, the country seat of President Andrew Jackson. While in this camp new winter clothing was issued and preparations were made for a winter campaign. Our life was without incident save the ordinary routine of camp life, drilling and going out after forage and keeping our quarters properly policed. Our last forage trip was on Christmas Day, and as usual the regiment had a skirmish, but came off without loss, returning to camp after night weary and march-worn. This trip was made on the Nolinsville Pike, going as far as Sheridan's old camping ground, where other troops joined us. The command, which seemed as large as a division, turned to the right and marched about ten miles, encountering a large body of rebel cavalry who showed fight, but retreated slowly and sullenly. The Fifty-first Indiana had some men wounded, and the Thirteenth Michigan one killed and two wounded.

Chapter Three

FROM NASHVILLE TO MURFREESBORO

On the morning of December 26th, 1862, tents were struck and everything packed for a forward march. The wagons, containing the tents and most of the baggage, with the sick and disabled, were sent to Nashville, while a few wagons with cooking utensils and hospital supplies and other essential things for use at headquarters went with the regiment. We marched about ten miles and camped near Lavergne.

We continued the march on the 27th to Stewart's, Creek, marching through the cedars in line of battle and driving the enemy before us most of the day in a drenching rain.

On the 28th, being Sunday, we remained in camp, starting again on Monday morning, the 29th, toward Murfreesboro, and that night our lines were in close proximity to those of the enemy. Just at dusk the command was given to Harker's Brigade to go forward to Murfreesboro, and this order was received with cheers, and the brigade started to cross Stone River in line of battle. The bed of the river was very stony and uneven, and sometimes a soldier would drop down in a hole until the water would be above his waist. The enemy's skirmish line opened a heavy musketry fire upon our troops, but the Seventy-third and the Fifty-fourth pushed forward and claimed the honor of being the first of the whole army to cross the river in the memorable battle about to be fought.

After the brigade was across it lined up and advanced, driving the enemy back until we were close up to the body of the rebel army. We could hear the commands of their officers, rallying their men and giving instructions. Our position was so perilous that an order was soon sent for us to withdraw and re-cross the river, and this order was silently and promptly executed and the regiment camped for the balance of the night after re-crossing the river, near its border, so close to the enemy that no camp fires could be built.

The weather was cold, and the boys suffered much from wet clothing. We afterwards learned that two of our men, Sebastian Lay, of Company B, and Charles Osborn, of Company E, were left asleep on the other side of the river and were made prisoners. They were later exchanged, and Lay returned to his company and Osborn was discharged and subsequently received a commission in the One Hundred and Twenty-Eighth Indiana.

On the morning of the 30th the enemy began firing artillery from the same position we had occupied the night before. Their shells came uncomfortably close, but did no damage in the brigade. Their missiles, going over our troops, struck a gun carriage in the rear, killing four men.

Our battery, the Sixth Ohio, opened fire on the enemy at this point and silenced their guns, but skirmishing continued in our front during the day, while there was heavy firing on some other parts of the line, especially to the right.

On the morning of the 31st the heavy fighting of this battle began. The regiment's quota of men for duty, according to the muster made that morning, was only 309, ten of whom were sick.

When the fighting began on the extreme right, Harker's Brigade was ordered to that point. Our regiment first occupied a position in the open woods about 200 yards southwest of the Nashville Pike. The Sixty-fifth Ohio was in our front and became hotly engaged, while our regiment lay in reserve with our brigade battery to the right. After a hot fight of some fifteen or twenty minutes the Sixty-fifth Ohio began to fall back through our ranks, and as soon as they were back of us Colonel Hathaway ordered our regiment to fire, and as rapidly as possible the fire was kept up for some time, and a bayonet charge was then made, driving the enemy back beyond the point where they had engaged the Sixty-fifth Ohio.

The Sixty-fourth Ohio then came up to our support. At this juncture four rebel regiments bore down on our left and opened a terrible enfilading fire, compelling us to fall back. Other regiments of our brigade came to our relief and the advance of the enemy was completely checked at this point. The day was far spent and the Seventy-third fell back in the cedars skirting the battle-field and prepared to spend the night in bivouac.

Here the teamsters under command of Quartermaster-Sergeant Williams, succeeded in bringing coffee and crackers to the men, and its effect was to waken up the tired, sleepy soldiers and set their tongues going with vigor, cheer and courage. We were not permitted, however, to remain in this sheltered position, and were ordered back into line in an open corn field, where we lay with our accoutrements on until morning.

Our regiment lost almost one-third of its men during this day's work, 92 out of the 309 men who went into action in the morning being killed, wounded or missing.

Company K lost half of the men with which it entered the fight. Colonel Hathaway's horse, "Redwood," was shot down under him, and he continued in command on foot.

Our regimental flag had nine bullet holes through it, and all the color-guards were shot down except Sergeant Hagherty, of Company D, who was the color-bearer.

On the morning of January 1st, 1863, about four o'clock, our brigade fell back a quarter of a mile and took position in the woods. About eight o'clock the enemy advanced in force, threatening our position, and coming on with a rebel yell, until stopped with a storm of shell, grape and canister from the Sixth Ohio Battery, which apparently quieted them until three o'clock in the afternoon, when their artillery opened fire on us.

Being protected by the trees and stones, the Seventy-third held its position without loss and remained on the ground until the morning of the 2nd, when an artillery battle was again fought between the Sixth Ohio Battery and the batteries of the enemy. In the confusion the Chicago Board of Trade Battery mistook the Sixth Ohio Battery for the enemy and opened fire on it, killing several horses and some of their gunners. The Thirteenth Michigan also suffered loss by the same mistake, it being in position to support the Sixth Ohio Battery.

Later the Seventy-third moved to the right, in open ground, and suffered much annoyance from sharpshooters posted in the woods. A line of skirmishers was thrown out and drove back the sharpshooters, when our men were compelled to fall back by a terrible artillery fire.

In the afternoon, about 4:30, the enemy began falling back, and the artillery kept up its work, our batteries responding until nearly dark. Colonel Harker's Brigade was then moved to the left and crossed the river to hold the ground which had been gained late in the afternoon.

During that night temporary breastworks, consisting of rails, poles, stones, and such things as could be found, were thrown up to afford protection, as an attack was expected next morning.

A drizzling rain set in, and next morning, January 3rd, the enemy failed to appear. We were then relieved by other troops and returned to the rear, where, we made coffee and obtained some rest. We had been in the front from the 29th of December to the morning of the 3rd of January, and we again took the front in the afternoon, but had no more engagements.

About midnight of the 3rd we were relieved from the front, and on the morning of the 4th we found that Murfreesboro had been evacuated by the enemy, and

General Rosecrans took possession.

In the afternoon our regiment went over to that part of the line where our desperate fight took place on December 31st, and gave three cheers for the victory.

General Rosecrans met us on our return and made a short speech, complimenting us very highly for the work we did and giving us the credit, in a great measure, of turning the tide of battle and saving the day.

The Seventy-third lost 27 killed, and from the best estimate that could be made the wounded and missing numbered 65, making a total of 92 killed, wounded and missing.

The following is the list of those killed in this battle:

Privates John H. Early and Edward Welch, of Company A;

Privates Hiram Babcock, John Brittenham, Ephraim T. Lane, William H. Moon and George Paul, of Company C;

Private Christopher Bucher, of Company D;

Captain Miles H. Tibbits and Privates Niles Singleton and Gilbert Weiner, of Company F;

Private Ephraim Powell, of Company G;

Captain Peter Doyle, Sergeant Henry H. Thornton, and Privates Samuel Burns and John H. Fiddler of Company H;

Sergeant William H. Hendee and Privates John Brown, Horace H. Curtis, George McCurdy, Thomas C. Shull, and Charles Stinchcomb, of Company I;

Corporal Carey I. Weston, color-guard, Wagoner Miles W. Peck, and Privates Christian Augustine, James McNally, William H. Peterson and Justice F. T. Stephens, of Company K.

The names of the wounded and missing will be found in the muster-out rolls of the respective companies.

After the battle we remained at Murfreesboro, changing one camp to another several times, until April 6th. During this time our duty was to guard forage trains, to go out on picket, to work on fortifications, guard supply trains to and from Nashville, and other similar duty.

On January 10th, Colonel Hathaway and Leander P. Williams, then acting as Quartermaster-Sergeant, started to Indiana, having leave of absence, and Captain Ivan N. Walker, of Company K, was left in command of the regiment. Lieutenant-Colonel Bailey having resigned December 22, 1862.

Captain Robert W. N. Graham, of Company I, was promoted to Lieutenant-Colonel, February 13th, 1863, and Captain Walker, of Company K, was promoted to Major.

Lieutenant-Colonel Graham being in ill health, never took command of the regiment, and resigned on March 29th, and on March 30th Major Walker was promoted to Lieutenant-Colonel.

Chapter Four

STREIGHT'S RAID

After the battle of Stones River, Colonel Abel D. Streight, of the Fifty-first Indiana Regiment, who was restless under enforced inaction, asked General Rosecrans, Commander of the Army of the Cumberland, to give him command of a Provisional Brigade, to be properly equipped and mounted, and charged with the duty of flanking Bragg's army, by the way of the Tennessee River, Northern Mississippi, Alabama and Georgia, for the purpose of interrupting, as far as possible, Bragg's communications south of Chattanooga by interfering with his transportation, destroying bridges and supplies, and such manufactories of army equipment as could be reached.

The commanding general, after some hesitation, finally granted Colonel Streight's request and gave him authority to organize such a brigade, permitting him to select four infantry regiments from the Army of the Cumberland and two companies of organized cavalry, all to be mounted and properly equipped for the undertaking.

After receiving his authority, Colonel Streight proceeded with his usual vigor to organize his brigade by selecting as his command his own regiment, the Fifty-first Indiana; the Seventy-third Indiana, Colonel Gilbert Hathaway; the Third Ohio, Colonel O. A. Lawson; the Eightieth Illinois, Lieutenant-Colonel A. F. Rodgers commanding; and Companies D and E of the First Middle Tennessee Cavalry, composed largely of loyal Alabamians, who had fled from that State as refugees into the Union lines, commanded by Captain David D. Smith, an intensely loyal Alabamian, and Captain Henry C. McQuiddy, a native of Shelbyville, Tennessee.

Colonel Streight at once commenced active preparation for his expedition by selecting as his staff: Captain D. L. Wright, of the Fifty-first Indiana, Assistant Adjutant-General;

Major W. L. Peck, Third Ohio, Brigade Surgeon; Lieutenant J. G. Doughty, Fifty-first, Brigade Quartermaster; Captain. E. M. Driscoll, Third Ohio, Brigade Inspector; Lieutenant C. W. Pavy, Eightieth Illinois, Brigade Ordnance Officer; and Lieutenant A. C. Roach, Fifty-first, Aide-de-Camp, all of whom were required to at once take charge of their respective positions and proceed as rapidly as possible to have everything ready for an early departure.

The brigade was ordered from Murfreesboro, Tennessee, to the city of Nashville, where supplies for its equipment were more abundant, and proceeded to make the change by railroad on the 6th day of April, 1863.

On arriving at Nashville requisitions for necessary equipments and supplies were at once issued and the preparation continued day and night until all was in readiness for departure except the animals on which to mount the command. These were scarce and of an inferior quality, and the failure to secure good ones greatly embarrassed the situation.

On the 10th of April, an order was received from General Rosecrans for the brigade to embark at once on the steamers then at the wharf at Nashville, as the press had already given out all the particulars they could ascertain as to destination and object of the expedition, which information, no doubt, was quickly sent into the rebel lines, Forest's Cavalry being then at Columbia, Tenn., fifty miles from Nashville, waiting and watching for an opportunity to strike a blow at the Union army or any detachment of it.

The boats were rapidly loaded and made ready for departure, and in the early dawn of the 11th left the wharf at Nashville and steamed down the Cumberland River with the Provisional Brigade on board, which arrived at Palmyra, Tenn., on the afternoon of that day, disembarked, and the Seventy-third ordered out for picket during a wet, cold and dreary night.

Palmyra had already suffered the ravages of war, and like many other small villages of that day, had been occupied by the contestants on each side until it was nothing but burnt and blackened ruins. The 12th was spent in efforts to gather in a supply of animals by a detail from the command for that purpose. Every horse and mule found were at once appropriated, as the command had left Nashville with less than 800, many of them useless for the service required. It was, therefore, imperative, if the expedition was to be a success, that this deficiency should be supplied.

The animals on hand were mostly unbroken and had to be tamed down before they could be of any service on the march. There was much fun and much danger experienced in this taming, as most of the mules when mounted would buck, jump stiff-legged, with head down and heels up, and over the rider would go. Fortunately no one was seriously hurt.

Colonel Streight was greatly mortified and chagrined that his Brigade Quartermaster had accepted such animals as were turned over to him at Nashville, and to show his estimate of them he reported to General Thomas as follows :

"The mules issued to me at Nashville were nothing but poor, wild, unbroken colts, many of them but two years old; a large number of them had the horse distemper; some forty or fifty of the lot were too near dead to travel and had to be left at the landing, and some ten or twelve died before we started. Those that were able to travel at all were so wild and unmanageable that it took nearly two days to catch and bridle them; even then a man saddling one was in great danger of his life unless he kept a sharp look-out for its heels."

On the 13th, Colonel Lawson, with four companies of the Third Ohio and three companies of the Seventy-third Indiana embarked for Fort Henry, on the Tennessee River, via Paducah, Ky., with all the equipments of the command on the eight transports that had brought the brigade to Palmyra. The balance of the command remained there during the day, selecting and breaking in the animals and foraging for more, with the result before stated.

On the 14th the balance of the brigade left Palmyra and marched fifteen miles, camped on Yellow Creek, fourteen miles from Fort Donelson (the scene of General Grant's first great success, and noted for his demand for "Unconditional Surrender.")

This was the first day's march as Mounted Infantry, though as yet only about one-third of the men, were mounted – a discouraging start for a command entering upon a most hazardous enterprise, and had it not been for the enthusiasm of the soldiers, who up to this time had known nothing but success in their military career, would have had a most depressing influence.

But the lovely spring weather, the bright flowers and foliage, and above all the novelty and excitement of the duty they were on, made them see the best side of the undertaking and the prospect of failure never entered their minds; but the fortunes of war are of all things the most variable.

The command reached Fort Henry on Wednesday the 15th of April, after a two days' march across the peninsula between Forts Donelson and Henry.

The transports had not reached Fort Henry when the command got there, but came up during the night, having been detained at Paducah, loading on supplies for General G. M. Dodge's army at Corinth, Mississippi.

Thursday, the 16th, was passed in getting the mules and horses aboard the boats. The number of these animals had greatly increased on our march, as the foragers had been industrious, and every old settler within ten miles of the road had contributed, though often unwillingly, all his serviceable animals to the "Mule Brigade." Many fine horses, as well as the best of mules, had thus been accumulated, and with the exception of not all being shod, were in good condition.

Having gotten all on board during the night, early on the morning of the 17th the fleet steamed up the beautiful Tennessee River, Major Walker with the right wing of the Seventy-third on board the steamer Baldwin, and Captain William M. Kendall, of Company D, with the left wing on the Aurora.

The 73rd regiment only numbered 303 men, being the smallest of the brigade. Colonel Ellett's Marine Fleet, organized to guard and patrol the Mississippi, Ohio, Tennessee and Cumberland rivers, escorted the transports to Eastport, Miss., where a landing was made in the afternoon of Sunday, the 19th.

Owing to low water, Eastport was the head of navigation for the large transports on which the brigade had come that far.

General Dodge had been ordered to advance in the direction of Tuscumbia, Ala., to cover and conceal, as far as possible, Colonel Streight's movements until he could break loose and get well on his way toward the railroad between Chattanooga and Atlanta, the main objective point of the expedition.

General Dodge's army was then in camp on Little Bear Creek, some ten miles distant from Eastport, to which Colonel Streight at once started for a consultation with General Dodge as to future movements.

Colonel Lawson, of the Third Ohio, was left in com mand of the brigade to direct and manage the landing of the animals and supplies. In doing so some 300 of the animals stampeded and succeeded in escaping into the woods.

Considerable time was lost in efforts to recapture the strays, but few, however, were recovered and a large share of them fell into the hands of the enemy. This was a great loss, as it caused a delay of two days at Eastport and further delay on reaching Tuscumbia to supply their places.

Left Eastport on the 21st of April, and made connection with General Dodge's command next day.

On the evening of the 22nd, Colonel Hathaway and Lieutenant L. P. Williams joined the Seventy-third.

They were in Indiana on detached duty when the regiment started from Nashville, and had considerable difficulty in joining the command, only succeeding in doing so by securing a tug at Paducah to take them to Eastport.

They brought with them about 15 or 20 men of the brigade who had been left behind.

On the next morning Colonel Hathaway took command of his regiment, relieving Major Ivan N. Walker, who had most satisfactorily commanded the Seventy- third during the absence of Colonel Hathaway.

Lieutenant Williams was at once detailed Acting Regimental Quartermaster, Lieutenant Edward Bacon, the Quartermaster, having been sent back on account of illness.

Before leaving camp, Colonel Streight, for the first time informed the brigade of the object and destination of the expedition, and in an order explained the perilous nature of the undertaking upon which we had started. That we would have to penetrate hundreds of miles into the enemy's country, would be surrounded by a wily foe for weeks, if successful, we would have to subsist entirely upon the country for rations that might be hard to obtain.

This information seemed only to quicken the spirits of the men and nerve them for the hardships of the march and brace them for the fighting which they now saw would have to come.

On the morning of the 23rd the march was continued toward Tuscumbia. General Dodge had the advance and cleared the road of such organized forces as showed themselves in his front.

Colonel Streight's scouts were scouring the country to secure animals to replace the ones lost at Eastport and were constantly skirmishing with the enemy who were hovering around trying to prevent foraging. They were not successful, however, as many horses and mules were secured, though they had to be fought for.

General Dodge reached Tuscumbia on the 24th,, where he found two regiments of Roddy's rebel cavalry, which he soon dispersed, and took possession of the town, a beautifully located place about four miles from the Tennessee river, surrounded by a very fertile country and noted for its famous springs of the purest water.

On the 25th General Dodge captured Florence, Ala., on the north side of the river, driving off about 1,500 rebel cavalry who were watching our movements and trying to prevent the collection of animals and supplies. From this day's work General Dodge turned over to Colonel Streight about 200 mules and six wagons. He also supplied him with 200 pack saddles, on which the men were expected to ride, being a most uncomfortable seat for them, as well as being hard on the backs of the animals.

The mules were as wild and unbroken as deer and many ludicrous scenes were witnessed and a number of the men hurt in trying to reduce their long-eared steeds to a state of gentleness.

The whole of the 25th and 26th of April was consumed in preparations for the start, and by ten o'clock of the night of the 26th there was some appearance of readiness.

About 150 of the men, however, were un-mounted, but the start could be delayed no longer and they must march on foot, depending upon the foragers to supply them. This was difficult to do, as the news of our raid having preceded us, most of the animals were so successfully concealed that but few were found.

Before daylight of the 27th of April the "Provisional Brigade" moved out of camp at Tuscumbia, Ala., in the direction of Rome, Georgia, which place, it was intended, should be reached as soon as possible.

General Dodge, to protect us, moved up the Tennessee river on our left flank to look after the enemy until we would be beyond their reach. But Forrest got the start of him and succeeded in crossing his command over the

Tennessee before he could be intercepted. This crossing at once placed the brigade on the defensive and greatly imperiled our hope of success.

During the day we passed through Russellville, Franklin County, Ala., where a rebel major was captured, who was sent back to General Dodge as a prisoner of war.

At night, after a march of thirty-four miles, encamped at Mount Hope, a small village in Lawrence County, Ala., a weary and exhausted lot of men and animals, as the route had been through a hilly country and over next to impassable roads.

Brigade headquarters were in the house of a wealthy secessionist who was bitter in his denunciation of the Union cause, but as an offset to his vituperation his daughter professed the warmest sympathy for the Union, and as a remuneration for her good wishes Colonel Streight ordered her to be paid for a saddle horse that she had claimed as her own which had been captured and appropriated by one of our "foot-back" soldiers.

This payment was made in accordance with General Rosecran's orders to pay all loyal citizens for supplies taken.

By order of Colonel Hathaway, Adjutant Wade, with Company G, went on a foraging tour to the plantation of Dr. Napier, who was in the rebel army. Large quantities of well cured meat and an abundance, of corn was found and taken, against the indignant protest of three handsome young ladies on the premises. The Adjutant, though a tender-hearted bachelor, did not listen to their entreaties, as he knew there were many hungry men in camp waiting for his return to appease their appetites.

The following day we reached Moulton, the county seat of Lawrence County, into which our cavalry, under Captain Smith, made a charge, capturing a number of Roddy's men and putting to flight the others.

The jail at Moulton was found crowded with natives of

Alabama who had been arrested and imprisoned because of their loyalty to their country and who had refused to be driven into the rebel army.

Many of these men were friends and acquaintances of Captain. Smith or his men, and a majority of them were natives of the county. On Captain Smith's request they were released from the prison, in which they had been held for months, and allowed to return to their homes, from where many of them finally reached our lines and entered the Union army.

Such was the persecution meted out to loyalty in that region by the Confederate authorities who had assumed control of a region which at the commencement of the war had been almost unanimously for the Union.

After a short stop at Moulton for refreshments and rest the march was resumed, it being evident that our success depended upon reaching Rome before Forrest could overtake us.

On the following day the foragers secured a sufficient number of animals to complete the mounting of the brigade, and for the first time the expedition was in condition to move rapidly.

We also captured during the day several wagons loaded with bacon, guns and ammunition, which were being taken to the rebel army. Such of these as could be made available for use were appropriated and the balance destroyed.

In the evening, April 29th, we reached the base of Sand Mountain and went into camp as the command was suffering for want of rest and sleep and the animals were greatly exhausted for want of feed. It was hoped that the next day would send us many miles on our road, although we had plenty of evidence that the enemy was rapidly concentrating and closing in upon us.

On the morning of the 30th, after a fairly good night's rest, an early start was made, and by daylight the brigade was on the move. The sun the rose through a clear sky and shone out bright and beautiful on a lovely spring day. As we moved out of camp and left the smoldering camp fires, the gray mist of the mountain tops sparkled like gems, and the scene was well calculated to inspire and encourage the weary soldiers; but alas, their hopes were not to be gratified, for soon after the column was on the move active skirmishing began between our rear guard and one of Roddy's regiments that had succeeded in reaching us.

It had been the hope of our commander to avoid a general engagement, if possible, and press forward with all haste to do the work for which the Provisional Brigade was organized; but the enemy was commanded by General N. B. Forrest, the most daring and experienced cavalry officer of the Confederate army in the southwest, who was as much determined to stop our progress as Colonel Streight was to continue it.

In this contention Forrest had the advantage, both in numbers of men and equipments, and could force a fight whether we wished it or not.

In carrying out his design he pressed our rear closely and brought his artillery into action, throwing shot and shell into our columns, and a battle was the only alternative.

As soon as a favorable position was obtained the brigade was halted and dismounted. The animals were taken to the rear and concealed as well as possible, every four of them under charge of one man.

A line of battle formed facing the approaching enemy, the Seventy-third on the left flank, reaching to the verge of a steep hill up which it was impossible for cavalry to charge; the Fifty-first on the right of the Seventy-third, with the Third Ohio and Eightieth Illinois occupying the right flank; the two pieces of artillery in the centre of the line; and the two companies of cavalry guarding the right and left flanks.

The whole line was at once ordered to lie down. In a short time Colonel Streight rode along the line giving orders and instructions to the regimental commanders. As he approached the Seventy-third Indiana, Colonel Hathaway saluted and awaited orders.

Colonel Streight said: "Colonel Hathaway, what do you think of charging the enemy when he comes to the top of the hill?" Colonel Hathaway replied: "Colonel, your orders, whatever they are, shall be obeyed." Colonel Streight, not quite satisfied with the reply, said : "But, Colonel Hathaway, I want to know what you think of making such a charge." Colonel Hathaway replied, "I think it would be a good move."

"Well, let it be done, then," said Colonel Streight, "and when the charge is made let it be done with a rush and as much noise as your men can make."

Colonel Hathaway walked along the line of his regiment and said to his officers, in the plain hearing of the men,

"Colonel Streight has ordered a charge to be made when the enemy comes to the top of the hill, and I want you, as soon as I give the order, to rise, take deliberate aim and fire, reload your guns as rapidly as possible, and when the order to charge is given, make a grand rush upon the enemy, firing at the same time, and yell in doing so as never men yelled before."

In about fifteen minutes the enemy appeared and gal⁻-; loped directly toward our line. When within about one hundred yards, Colonel Hathaway gave the order to rise, fire, and charge the rebel line, which was done with such energy that numbers of them were killed and wounded, their line broken into fragments, causing a hasty retreat down the hill.

As soon as they could reform another charge was made upon the Seventy-third and Fifty-first, which was repulsed with greater slaughter than the first.

By this time the Third Ohio and Eightieth Illinois were engaged and made a furious charge against the enemy, capturing two pieces of artillery. The cheers of the brave Union boys sounded loud and long as the enemy gave way, running in great disorder, pursued for some distance by our men, who were recalled and the line of battle re-established

The captured guns were manned by details from the different regiments and everything made ready for another attack, which did riot come, as the enemy was so crippled that it could not then renew the offensive.

The rebel loss was about 150 officers and men killed

and wounded, including Captain W. H. Forrest, a brother of the General. About thirty prisoners were captured and later in the day paroled.

Our brigade's loss in killed and wounded was 31 officers and men. Among the killed was Lieutenant-Colonel James W. Sheets, of the Fifty-first Indiana, who fell while leading his regiment in a charge. Lieutenant Charles W. Pavey, Eightieth Illinois, Brigade Ordnance Officer, was dangerously wounded in the back by a fragment of shell. He finally recovered and joined his comrades in Libby Prison.

The loss of the Seventy-third was Robert Jackson, Company E, killed.

Two of Company K's men, Henry Bird and Shannon. Carr, had left the command early in the morning as foragers, and about the time of the engagement were captured by Roddy's men, who turned them over to a squad of guerillas, calling themselves Home Guards, and by them were taken into a lonely ravine, where they were deliberately murdered.

This horrible butchery was seen by one of our cavalrymen, a native of Alabama, who was expecting a similar fate, but by a bold dash succeeded in escaping and more than fifteen months afterwards told the writer about this slaughter.

Corporal J. J. Ferris, of Company K, was struck by pieces of shell which severed his left arm near the shoulder, and all the fingers of his right hand were completely cut off.

A minie ball passed through the body of A. C. Foot, Comany F, cutting the lower lobe of the left lung. These men were left on the battleground and were afterwards taken care of by Union people of the neighbor-hood, treated by a citizen doctor, finally recovered, and returned to our lines.

We remained on the field for some time, anticipating a second attack from the enemy, who, we ascertained, were being rapidly reinforced by the arrival of Forrest's entire command. He did not, however, renew the attack during our occupation of this position.

The best arrangement possible was made for the care

of our wounded, whom we were compelled to leave in a field hospital hastily established and placed in charge of Dr. William Spencer, Assistant Surgeon of the Seventy-third Indiana Regiment, who was supplied with such articles for their comfort and sustenance, together with medicines and surgical instruments, as could be spared.

The treatment of our wounded after the enemy advanced was inhuman and brutal beyond expression. Every ounce of the bread, meat, sugar, coffee, etc., left for them was immediately taken possession of by Forrest's unfeeling troopers and appropriated to their own use. All blankets and clothing that they could seize were also taken, leaving our wounded without coverings of any kind, or garments to protect them from the mountain breezes. Their hats were taken from their heads, and shoes from their feet, sometimes dropping their own dilapidated hats and shoes, calling it an "even swap." These unfeeling robberies of wounded and defenceless men were often done in the presence of rebel officers who did not make the slightest effort to prevent it, but, on the other hand, appeared to sanction it.

These scenes only terminated when our men had been robbed of everything they possessed, including pocket knives, combs and other small though useful articles.

Even the medicines, dressings, and surgical instruments left with Dr. Spencer for the benefit of our wounded were taken by the rebel surgeons and carried off.

Consequently our men had to lie with their undressed wounds and suffer until death put an end to their misery, several of them dying, who, with kind treatment and attention would have recovered.

The loyal citizens of the vicinity would have gladly assisted in the care of the stricken ones and given them all the relief in their power had they been permitted to do so, but not even a cup of milk or a piece of bread was allowed to be given them by these sympathizing friends, and it was only when the vigilance of the guards could be evaded that our wounded could receive the slightest favor from this source.

Nor were these wounded prisoners of war the only victims of this persecution. Citizens who were suspected of loyalty to the Union were compelled to suffer indignities and inhuman treatment by their oppressors. Mrs. Penn, a widow of the vicinity, who had two sons in Captain Smith's Alabama Cavalry, was visited with the greatest indignities. She and her daughter were driven from their home, their property taken, their houses and fences burned and growing crops destroyed.

Colonel Streight, learning that Forrest was rapidly concentrating his forces nearby, as soon as he could partially provide for the wounded, and about two hours after the battle, decided to pull away and proceed on the march.

The brigade was mounted and pushed ahead, leaving Day's Gap several miles in the rear, without feeling any pursuit until about four o'clock p. m., when our rear was again attacked, and as we did not want to lose time by halting to give battle if it could be avoided the column was kept in motion, skirmishing going on, however, all the time between Captain Smith's Cavalry companies and the enemy's advance. Owing to the superior numbers they made it very difficult for Captain Smith with his handful of men to keep them at bay; but he succeeded in doing so for over two hours.

They were now pressing us so closely that Colonel Streight, after consultation with Colonel Hathaway and the other regimental commanders, resolved to halt the command and again give battle as soon as a good position, could be reached.

About sundown we came to Crooked Creek, the crossing of which was found tedious owing to the delay in doing so to allow the thirsty animals to drink. The enemy pressed us severely, and came near cutting off the Third Ohio, which was bringing up the rear.

After crossing, Colonel Hathaway took the Seventy-third into position, where it dismounted, formed into line, advanced a short distance, and poured a heavy volley into the enemy's ranks, stopping them long enough for the Third

Ohio to cross and get into line with the rest of the brigade, which Colonel Streight had so formed as to cover the crossing, deploying up and down the stream in such a way as to prevent the enemy reaching the ford.

The contestants lined up on each side of Crooked Creek commenced a fierce engagement along the lines, and although the enemy was in much greater numbers than our brigade their aim was bad, firing over our heads and doing but little harm.

This engagement raged with great desperation for some time, and being now dark, the flashes from musketry and artillery lit up the hills and woods with the battle's glare, and made a scene of grandest sublimity.

About nine o'clock we discovered the enemy had begun to waver and fall back. In a short time all was quiet.

Our little howitzers did good work, as did the two captured guns until their ammunition gave out, when they were spiked, cut down and abandoned.

Although the enemy was in greatly superior force at this engagement the advantage was on our side as the foe was compelled to withdraw and leave us in possession of the ground we had first occupied. The little brigade had thus won two battles in one day over a very determined enemy whose object was to stop our progress and bring us to grief as soon as possible.

The Seventy-third lost no men in this battle, but the brigade lost a number, among them the brave and gallant young Adjutant of the Eightieth Illinois, Lieutenant J. C. Jones.

Two of the medical staff, Dr. Peck, Brigade Medical Director, and Dr. King, had remained on the field, assisting to care for the wounded until a rebel regiment had formed and started in pursuit. They rode the whole length of the column without exciting suspicion until they had reached the head, when they made a dash, which attracted attention at once, and they were ordered to halt. Not obeying this command they were fired upon and pursuit made. A trial of speed took place. Dr. Peck, being splendidly mounted, outran his pursuers and soon joined our command, but Dr. King was overtaken and made a prisoner.

Dr. Peck's arrival gave the information that pursuit had commenced, and while in passing through a heavy body of timber Colonel Hathaway was directed to halt the Seventy-third; conceal themselves in the woods, and ambush the enemy.

In a short time they appeared, and as the advance battalion came up within about forty yards of our concealed regiment a volley of musketry was poured into them which stopped their advance and sent them back pell mell in consternation and disorder. They withdrew for quite a distance and contented themselves in shelling the woods for some time, thus giving the Seventy-third an opportunity to rejoin the command.

The rebels having the advantage of a close knowledge of the roads, as well as in numbers of men, soon rallied and attacked us again about two o'clock in the morning.

Another ambush was ordered, which proved so successful that we had no further annoyance during the night.

Our course continued in a southwest direction, farther and farther toward Rome, Ga., which showed we were not fleeing' from the enemy but intent on the original object of our expedition.

After the last repulse of the enemy in the night we had traveled at a lively pace until about eight o'clock a.m., May 1st, we arrived at Blountsviile, Ala., where we halted for rest and feed, as both men and animals were greatly famished and fatigued as they had had but little rest for two days and nights.

The wagon train had greatly impeded our progress, and it was here determined to reduce it and dispense with all but one wagon. The others were piled up and burned. The necessary baggage and supplies were placed on pack mules and given to the teamsters who were charged with their guidance and care.

Of all the men in the Seventy-third we had but one who had had experience in loading a pack mule and tying the "diamond hitch," and that one was Colonel Hathaway himself, who in several trips he had made in Texas with trains of pack mules had learned the rather complicated art of properly securing baggage on these refractory animals.

He called his teamsters up, and in a short time taught them how to do this job, with the result that there was less trouble with the pack train of the Seventy-third than that of any of the other regiments of the brigade.

By this time a large cavalcade of negroes were bent on following us, thinking we had come among them for their deliverance. Their presence delayed us and became such an impediment that Colonel Streight was compelled to issue an order prohibiting them in our lines as they greatly impeded our march and made our own defence much more difficult.

As we were leaving Blountsville, about 11 o'clock a.m., our pickets were attacked by Forrest's advance, which was held back for about one hour by our cavalry, under Captains Smith and McQuiddy, giving the brigade that much start. The cavalry, seeing great danger of being surrounded and captured, withdrew at a lively gait, and even then Captain Smith lost ten of his men who could not get away.

The enemy renewed its efforts and pressed us so hard that on coming to Black River, where the fording was very difficult, the whole brigade dismounted and drove them back at the point of the bayonet before we could cross. This checked them and we moved on until midnight, when the exhaustion was so great that a little rest must be had or else the men and animals would fall by the wayside, so we dismounted in the woods for feed and rest.

It now became plain that our expedition could not accomplish the task set for it, nor could we reach our own lines in safety, and the only thing to do was to press on as far as possible and do what we could against their military resources.

Left our camp in the woods at an early hour in the morning of May 2nd, the Seventy-third in advance. A short time after sunrise we reached Black Creek near Gadsden, Ala., crossed on a fine wooden bridge, which was burned by our rear guard, hoping to delay Forrest's forces long enough for us to reach Rome before he could again overtake us, as the stream was very deep and seemed un-fordable.

But among a lot of prisoners we had captured that morning was one well acquainted with the river, who, as soon as he was set at liberty, made his way direct to Forrest and piloted that officer and his command to a ford where they crossed and again were in pursuit.

Reaching Gadsden, Etowah County, Ala., on the Coosa River, about 10 a. m., several rebel officers were captured and a large quantity of provisions in store for the enemy were found and destroyed. Also about two hundred guns were captured. It was expected that a small steamer could be found on which a detachment could be sent against Rome, but there was none there.

Owing to the great efforts that had been made to evade Forrest the animals were now greatly exhausted, and after destroying the bridge over Black Creek our progress was slow and tedious, but the enemy being delayed by the loss of the bridge, we were not attacked until after we reached Blount's Farm, where, finding plenty of forage, a halt was made to feed.

Before the men could get anything prepared for themselves, about 4 p. m., the pickets were vigorously attacked.

Company G had been detailed as videttes, and received the bulk of the charge. The Seventy-third rushed at once to their assistance by forming in line across the road, and succeeded in breaking the force of the attack, while Colonel Streight got the balance of the brigade in line and met their advance with success.

Our loss had not been great, and Colonel Hathaway left Adjutant Wade with the right wing of the Seventy-third while he rode over to the left, where Major Walker was in command, and immediately after giving directions and encouraging the men, the howitzers doing great execution, a minie ball struck Colonel Hathaway, pierced his breast, and before anyone could get to him he fell from his horse mortally wounded.

He was carried to Blount's Farm, examined by Dr. Myers, our surgeon, who did all that was possible for him. He was unable to utter a word, soon became unconscious, and in less than an hour from the time he was stricken, expired.

The fatal bullet had been fired by a sharpshooter, who, as soon as he saw the effects of his shot, jumped from his concealment; but he did not have a moment to rejoice over his deed for half a hundred guns were leveled on him, with the result that his life passed away before that of his noble victim.

Colonel Hathaway had, from the time of his joining his regiment and the brigade, on the 22nd day of April, conducted himself in the most gallant and heroic manner, doing everything there was in his power to make our expedition a success and showing that determined and loyal spirit that did not for one moment shrink from the duty that he recognized was his.

As the sun set on that tranquil evening, sinking slowly down behind the forest, unstirred by the least breath of wind, the conflict ceased for the day. But the noble, chivalric Hathaway was no more. He fell, the noblest of sacrifices on the altar of his country, to whose glorious service he had dedicated his life, and thus passed away a noble, lofty soul.

Thus ended a career full of arduous and splendid achievement. He was ever with that part of his regiment which was under the hottest fire, and when the enemy shifted their fire to other portions he proceeded thither and directed the movements of each company in person.

His men will remember how cheering and inspiring was his presence with them in the most exciting moments, and his brave, cheerful voice was the herald of success. His character was so frank and open and beautiful, and his bearing so modest and full of sympathy that he conciliated all hearts and made everyone who met him his friend.

Thus, modest, brave, loving and beloved, the famous, the good citizen, the charming companion, he was called away from the scenes of his triumphs and glory to a brighter world, where neither war nor rumors of war ever come, and wounds and pain and suffering are unknown.

The crisis with our brigade was rapidly approaching. The next few hours must decide the fate of our expedition. We were not more than one day's hard march from Rome, where we had hoped to cross the Coosa River, destroy the bridge, and thus effectually stop pursuit, giving time to recruit the exhausted energies of the command, gain a fresh supply of animals and rations, and possibly a supply of ammunition.

In order to facilitate this hoped for success a detail was made of 200 of our best mounted men, under command of Captain Milton Russell, of the Fifty-first, who were ordered to march to Rome as rapidly as possible, take possession of the bridge, armories, manufactories and warehouses containing supplies, and hold them until the arrival of the balance of the brigade. If they could not be so held, destroy them and fall back on the main command.

As soon as this detachment was off, the enemy not pressing, the command was ordered to follow in its wake.

All but the Seventy-third mounted and started. Major Walker, now in command, withdrew the right wing, leaving the left under Adjutant Wade, still facing the foe. By this time it was dark, and the enemy showing signs of again attacking, the Adjutant marched back with his command and set fire to two large buildings in our front, which lit up the surrounding country, but the rebels, not wishing to encounter an ambuscade, held aloof and did not advance.

By eight o'clock the entire command was again on the march, weary and greatly exhausted from the continuous exertions of the past five days and nights, not having more than two hours' sleep and rest at any one time during that period.

The brigade continued to march all night, not halting till 8 o'clock a.m., May 3rd. About 12 o'clock at night the sky was illuminated by a great conflagration, caused by the burning of the Round Mountain Iron Works, in Cherokee County, Ala., an immense manufactory of ordnance and army equipments run by the confederate government. One of our scouting parties had put the match to it and succeeded in destroying this valuable factory and its machinery, together with a great quantity of finished and unfinished material, and it was not again put in operation during the war.

This night ride can never be forgotten by the participants. They were so used up for the want of sleep that it seemed almost impossible to keep awake, and they were so weak for want of food that many reeled in their saddles as the mules jogged along, themselves exhausted from fatigue and want of food.

By the mistake of a guide several hours were lost in finding the right ford over the Chattooga River, causing a serious delay and taking us ten or twelve miles out of the way.

Thus the night wore away, and the morning of Sunday, May 3, 1863, Gaylesville, Ala., found an army of what had but lately been a stalwart lot of men, unable longer to cope with the superior force.

A halt was ordered, the animals fed, and an effort made to prepare a breakfast for the famished men, but scarcely had a bite been eaten when a volley from the pickets nearby told that the enemy was again at hand.

Orders were given to fall into line, to do which now required considerable effort. Our ammunition for the artillery and musketry was in bad shape from dampness, and another contest looked very discouraging.

Still, the will to do or die was there, and the men rallied and fell into line as quickly as circumstances would permit, ready for another engagement.

Some skirmishing took place between the .rebel advance and our skirmishers, when, Forrest arriving, sent a flag of truce to Colonel Streight, demanding a surrender.

Colonel Streight held a consultation with the regimental commanders, in which our situation and chances of success were fully canvassed. We had but a small quantity of artillery ammunition, and the few rounds of rifle and musket cartridges on hand were almost entirely unfit for service. The enemy had a brigade on our left endeavoring to flank us, and had, in fact, at that time almost accomplished it. We had no news from Captain Russell as to the result of his dash on Rome.

General Forrest, having the .advantage of better mounts, had been able to rest his command at least half of each night. His soldiers were therefore fresh and vigorous compared with ours.

It was evident that we had to contend with a superior force, both in front and rear. All things taken into consideration, our situation seemed hopeless, and the conference therefore decided to surrender on the following terms:

"First - each regiment should be permitted to retain its colors. Second - the officers were to retain their side-arms. Third - both officers and men were to retain their haversacks, knapsacks and blankets, and all private property of any description was to be respected and retained by its owner. Fourth - both officers and men were to be paroled and sent north within ten days."

General Forrest agreeing with these terms, Colonel Streight explained to the men the terms and the necessity of our surrender. Our brigade was then drawn up in line, arms stacked, and we were prisoners of war.

After allowing an hour or two for rest and food, we were marched under guard to Rome in a manner very different from the way we had hoped to enter that city, but as we had done all it was possible to do to have our way, we trust no one ever thought it was our fault that we did not succeed.

On the road to Rome we met Captain Russell's detachment, who reported that about eight o'clock on that morning of May 3rd, after riding all night, he had reached the outskirts of the city and found the bridge over the Coosa River already well guarded and the city and adjoining country full of armed men, Forrest having dispatched a citizen from Gadsden by a much shorter route than we had taken to give the alarm and notify them of our approach.

This had prevented any show of success by Captain Russell, who, after considerable ineffectual skirmishing between his men and the enemy's pickets, had fallen back intending to rejoin the main command, which he now met as prisoners. His detachment having been included in the general surrender, returned with us to Rome.

The terms of our surrender were lenient, and were not violated while we were under General Forrest's jurisdiction, but as soon as we were separated from his command not a single item of them seemed to have any binding force upon the confederate authorities.

Our captors were considerate of our feelings, indulged in no tantalizing expressions or rejoicing, and expressed themselves as glad that the chase was over, and freely acknowledged that we had made a most gallant and determined defense, and if we had been as well mounted as they, would no doubt have succeeded in our undertaking.

Forrest's Adjutant, Major Charles W. Anderson, told one of our officers who had been acquainted with him before the war that when they left Columbia, Tenn., they were the best mounted command in the confederacy, but so determined had been our defense that their strength was gone, their loss great, and it would take months of rest to recuperate from their exhaustion. So it was plain that we had given them as hard blows as we had received.

The officers were separated from the enlisted men, and in company with Forrest and staff reached Rome that evening and were quartered in the Etowah House, where most of them slept on the floor. The enlisted men camped by the way in an open field. Having no guard duty to do gave their tired bodies and minds a good undisturbed night's rest.

Next day, May 4th, they marched to Rome and were corralled in an open lot, with no shelter whatever from the broiling sun. On their march they were reviewed by citizens, who lined the road curious to see the "Yankees," this being the first command to penetrate so far into their country.

Many of them were very insolent and disagreeable. The guards were otherwise, being courteous and respectful, showing the difference between "stay-at-homes" and those in actual service.

The rations furnished the prisoners were inadequate and consisted of a meager chunk of boiled fat pork and a small piece of very poor corn bread, but as bad as it all was everybody took it good naturedly, entering into friendly talk, exchanging jokes and experiences with the guards.

Paroles were made out and signed on the 4th, the officers transferred from the hotel to less commodious quarters, and the enlisted men held in the open lot under a strong guard.

On the 5th the whole of the brigade was transferred to Atlanta, Ga., a distance of over seventy miles, in poor and dirty freight cars. The officers, about 100 in number, including surgeons and chaplains, were quartered in the City Hall, and rations were furnished from a hotel, for which they were required to pay for two days' supply over $1,200.

On Thursday, the 7th, they were removed to a military prison in the centre of the city, a very uncomfortable and overcrowded place. The rations were now furnished by the authorities and were of a miserable character, consisting of corn bread and beef, unpalatable and scarce.

Four days of discomfort were passed in this hot hole. Sunday, May 10th, was devoted largely to religious service. The Chaplains of the Eightieth Illinois, Third Ohio, and Chaplain Frazier of the Seventy-third each preaching a sermon during the day and evening.

Upon their arrival in Atlanta the enlisted men were

again corralled in an open field without shelter, or even blankets or overcoats, they having all been taken from them.

The weather turned suddenly very cold and wet. Not enough wood was furnished to cook the scanty rations furnished, much less to keep the men the least bit warm or in anywise comfortable. Their sufferings while remaining there were extreme, and many have said that with all the hardships of their entire service no time equaled the days spent at Atlanta.

On Thursday, the 7th of May, they were escorted to the railroad, placed in rickety box cars, and started for Richmond by the East Tennessee route. The whole journey was one of unmitigated hardship and starvation, the cars crowded to suffocation, refreshing sleep impossible, and not an incident occurring to relieve the situation over the whole distance except that the guards were as lenient toward the prisoners as their orders would permit.

This dismal journey ended on or about May 11th, 1863, by their arrival at Richmond, and were immediately transferred to Belle Isle Prison, located on a small island in the James River, in plain sight of the city of Richmond.

This prison had already become notorious from the inhuman treatment accorded to those confined there. The treatment of the men of the "Provisional Brigade" was in no wise an improvement over what others had endured there.

The only amelioration was that their paroles were not entirely ignored, and on the morning of Saturday, May 16th, they were ordered into line and escorted to City Point, transferred to the Flag of Truce boat, received with honor under the stars and stripes, furnished with the best of good and wholesome food - something they had not enjoyed for weeks, and in a happy mood transferred to Parole Camp at Annapolis, Md., where an outfit of new clothing was furnished them.

Chapter Five

FROM ANNAPOLIS TO INDIANAPOLIS

The Indiana regiments, after receiving their new clothing at Annapolis, were in a few days removed to Camp Chase, Columbus, Ohio, and being detained there for some time, numbers of the men became so eager to see their families and friends that they could not wait the slow process of securing furloughs, and several took "french leave," and after displaying considerable tact in avoiding provost guards on the cars and highways, reached their homes and for a few days enjoyed themselves very much; but soon all returned to their duties after their stolen vacation.

The Fifty-first and Seventy-third Indiana Regiments, about May 25th, 1863, were transferred from Parole Camp, Columbus, Ohio, to Camp Carrington, Indianapolis, Indiana, and given furloughs for 15 days to their homes. This time was spent in a most happy reunion with relatives and friends and went a long way to remove the sting of a military failure and the un- pleasantness of prison life.

On the expiration of the furloughs all returned to Indianapolis, and having been declared exchanged, moved their quarters to Camp Morton to guard rebel prisoners who were confined in that camp.

There they had a good opportunity to compare their own hardship in southern prisons with the comfortable manner which southern prisoners were treated in northern prisons.

The Seventy-third remained at Indianapolis for several months, commanded at different times by Captains John H. Beeber, of Company D, and Emanuel M. Williamson, of Company I.

General John Morgan, of the Southern Army, during the summer organized a raid to overrun Kentucky, Indiana and Ohio and do all the damage he could to the loyal people of those States. To meet this emergency Governor Morton ordered General O. B. Wilcox, who was in command of that military district, to assemble all his troops to meet Morgan wherever he might show himself. This made it necessary for the Seventy-third again to enter the field.

On the night of July 4th the "long roll" was sounded in camp, and the Seventy-third at once fell into line. Three days' rations were ordered to be drawn and all be ready to march at 7 o'clock a.m.

At that hour the troops boarded a train on the Jeffersonville railroad, which in good time reached the Ohio River and crossed to Louisville, Ky., where much excitement prevailed. The Seventy-third was ordered at once to take up its march for the Bardstown Pike. About four miles out camp was formed, and the Seventy-third ordered on picket. During the night some little excitement arose, caused by the approach of two carriages loaded with Union officers, who, having the proper countersign, were admitted, but did not disclose to the wondering pickets the object of their night excursion.

The regiment remained in this camp two days, when, getting word that Morgan had crossed the river and was then in Indiana, the command returned to New Albany. From there they went to Corydon, which place Morgan had captured. In the morning he had fled. The Seventy-third took the rear chase, and coming onto his rear guard, had a skirmish which resulted in no loss to the Union boys, but some to Morgan, both as to horses and men.

From Corydon the regiment returned to Jeffersonville and took boats there for Cincinnati, accompanied by a fleet of boats loaded with men and cannon. It remained in Cincinnati but a few hours, and then went up the river to Portsmouth, Ohio. The regiment made several brief stops; the most important was at Maysville, Ky.

On reaching Portsmouth it was immediately transferred to R. R. train and started for Otway, Ohio, which

Morgan was trying to reach. On learning that troops were nearby he flanked the town and moved on.

That night his camp fires were in sight. Before daylight next morning he had "skedaddled," as his career was drawing to a close, and danger of capture was imminent unless he could cross the Ohio and get into Kentucky, which he considered a more hospitable region for him than the loyal soil of Ohio. His capture occurred a few hours afterwards and the Seventy-third's chance for an engagement with the raiders had passed.

Returning to Portsmouth, boats were taken to Madison, Indianapolis, entered their quarters at Camp Morton, and resumed the duty of guarding southern prisoners, which was monotonously continued until late in October, 1863, when the regiment was relieved and ordered to Nashville, Tenn, with the hope that it could there be concentrated, and the officers, who were yet in prison, be exchanged and returned to their commands.

This last hope was disappointed, as none but the three who afterwards escaped from Libby Prison and the two who were specially exchanged, reached the regiment in time to see any active service, as the war was over before they were released.

Publishers note: It should be made clear here... that at the end of Streight's Raid, after surrender near Rome, GA, enlisted men of the 73rd and other Regiments of the Brigade were exchanged and back in Indiana in about a month, as described in Chapter Five above.

However, the officers of the 73rd and those of all Regiments in the Brigade were held in imprisonment, most of them for the rest of the War. Chapter Six is their story.

Chapter Six

LIBBY PRISON

The officers left Atlanta on Monday, May 11, 1863, at 7 o'clock p. m., in dirty and dilapidated box cars, hardly fit for transportation of cattle, arriving at Augusta, .Ga. 8 a.m., May 12th.

In the afternoon they started by railroad to Columbia, S.C., which was reached next morning at daylight.

After marching through the city they embarked for Charlotte, N.C., which was reached about 3 o'clock p.m., over a very rough railroad. No rations were received here, notwithstanding there was a warehouse full of provisions near the depot. They were loaded on open cars, with cross ties for seats, and transported on very slow time to Raleigh, N. C. During the day they stopped at a place named Company's Shops, about half way, where they got a very poor dinner for $2 apiece. Reached Raleigh 9 o'clock p.m. on the t4th, and were furnished with a few hard crackers, a very inadequate ration,

Left Raleigh about 11 p.m., and arrived at Weldon, N. C., on the morning of the 15th, and continued directly on for Petersburg, Va., arriving there late in the afternoon.

We were kept waiting in the street for several hours, and were finally taken into a small brick building into which all were crowded, with scarcely room to lie down.

Early in the morning we were moved to Richmond, Va., a distance of 22 miles, which was reached in the forenoon. We were held at the depot under guard some time and then marched to the front of Libby Prison. While waiting on the sidewalk those fortunate enough to have money succeeded in buying a little bread at $1 for a small loaf.

We entered Libby Prison about 3 o'clock p.m., May 16, 1863, where a strict search of each person was made for money or other valuables, and what had failed to escape the sharp eyes of the searchers at Atlanta was here found and taken.

All of the officers of Streight's command were then sent to the upper rooms of the prison, where were found about 100 officers that had been captured on the 3rd day of May at Chancellorsville, awaiting exchange, and Captain Samuel McKee, of the Fourth Kentucky Cavalry, held as a hostage, and A. D. Richardson and Junius Henri Brown, war correspondents of the "New York Tribune," and Richard T. Colburn of the "New York World," all of whom were captured on the Mississippi River on the 3rd day of May in front of Vicksburg, while attempting to pass the rebel batteries. Mr. Colburn was soon released as a favor to the "World" newspaper, which at that time was an apologist for secession, if nothing worse.

Richardson and Brown were held as citizen prisoners, removed from Libby Prison to Castle Thunder, a vile hole, and from thence to Salisbury, N.C., from which place, after months of imprisonment, they made their escape and reached the Union lines at Knoxville, Tenn., after a month or more of great suffering and privation.

Captain McKee was held until the end of the war and released with the other captured officers.

On the night of February 9th, 1864, Colonel Streight and Captains W. W. Scearce and William Wallick of the Fifty-first Regiment, Captain Matt Boyd of Company F Seventy-third, and Lieutenant William Reynolds and Lieutenant L. P. Williams of Company K Seventy-third, escaped from the prison by the way of the famous tunnel and safely reached the Union lines at Williamsburg, Va., after near a week of almost unheard of suffering from the severe cold weather and hunger which they had to endure.

Major Walker and Captain I. D. Phelps escaped, but were retaken close to the Union lines.

Captain Marion T. Anderson, of the Fifty-first, had previously, in company with Captain Skelton of an Iowa regiment, escaped from the hospital at Libby by bribing one of the prison guards.

Lieutenant-Colonel Ivan N. Walker and Major A. B. Wade were specially exchanged. All the other officers of the Seventy-third remained prisoners until the rebellion had fallen.

Captain David D. Smith, of Alabama, one of the officers of our cavalry companies, was taken from Libby Prison upon a requisition of the Governor of Alabama, on a charge of disloyalty to his native state, and carried from one county prison to another all over Alabama until July, 1865, long after the war was over, when he was sent to Annapolis, where, owing to his deplorable condition, he survived but a few days. His friends never learned the particulars of his prison life in Alabama. Thus perished one of those southern heroes, whose only offence was his true and loyal devotion to the flag of his country. He died a martyr to the cause of the Union.

The remaining officers of Streight's brigade were prisoners about twenty-three months from the time of their capture, May 3rd, 1863, to April 1st, 1865.

They were kept in Libby for over a year, then removed to Danville, Va., where they were held but a brief time, thence to Columbia, S. C., Macon, Ga., Savannah, Ga., and Charleston, S. C.

At the latter city, with hundreds of others, they were placed under the fire of the guns of General Gilmore, who was then bombarding Charleston. The Confederate authorities notified General Gilmore that the prisoners had been so placed, hoping it would stop the firing on the city. During several months not a prisoner was injured, though the shelling was regularly continued.

After General Sherman's march to the sea the Confederates found their prisons no longer tenable and began sending Union prisoners into our lines, and by the time of Lee's surrender very few were left in the South.

The officers of the Seventy-third, upon reaching

Annapolis, at once reported to the War Department in Washington and were granted thirty days' leave of absence and furnished with transportation to their homes.

Before their leave expired the following tendered their resignations and were honorably discharged from the service, as of the 15th of May, 1865; Adjutant James C. Woodrow, Lieutenant John W. Munday, Company B., Lieutenant Henry H. Tillotson, Company E; Lieutenant Robert J. Connelly, Company G; Lieutenant Andrew M. Callahan, Company H.

The following officers, at the end of their leave, rejoined the regiment on the 15th of May, 1865, namely: Major William M. Kendall, Captain.Alfred Fry, Lieutenant H. Ralph Uptigrove, Company A; Captain John A. Richley, Lieutenant Alexander N. Thomas, Company C; Lieutenant John L. Brown, Company E; Captain Horace Gamble, Company F; Captain Joseph A. Westlake, Company G; Captain Daniel H. Mull and Lieutenant Henry S. Murdock, Company H; Lieutenant Adolphus H. Booher, Company I; and Captain Ithamer D. Phelps, Company K.

They were joyfully received and welcomed by their command and remained with the regiment during the rest of its service and were honorably mustered out with the regiment at Nashville on the 1st day of July, 1865.

These brave men had undergone the most protracted imprisonment and remarkable escape from death of any Union prisoners during the war.

All honor to their bravery, their endurance, and their steadfast loyalty during the most trying ordeals which men were ever called to meet.

Chapter Seven

DETACHMENT SERVING WITH THE SIXTY-FIFTH OHIO

Before taking up the story of the regiment subsequent to the raid and capture and imprisonment of its officers, we will give an account of a detachment that served with the Sixty-fifth Ohio in the campaign against Chattanooga in 1863.

This account is taken from the original paper prepared by Sergeant Job Barnard, of Company K, at the request of Colonel Wade, and which paper was found among his effects, and endorsed in Colonel Wade's handwriting, as follows :

"Headquarters Seventy-third Indiana, Larkinsville, Ala., March 31, 1865."

"Barnard, Job, First Sergeant Company K, Seventy-third Indiana."

"History of Seventy-third Company, temporarily attached to 65th Ohio Volunteers, to be incorporated in history of Seventy-third Indiana."

On the 21st of April, 1863, when Colonel Streight was preparing to leave Eastport, Miss., on his raiding mission all those thought by the brigade surgeon unable to stand the hardships of the campaign were set aside and ordered on board the steamer La Crosse to return with the transports and marine fleet to Paducah.

We were all finally stowed away, though not the most comfortably, and came down to Hamburg, where we lay over until noon of the next day. Here we met and saw for the first time Colonel Hathaway, who was on his way with Lieutenant Williams to join the regiment. They had come up the river in the little steam tug Cleveland, and General Ellet sent them on to East Port in one of the gunboats.

We made but slow progress down the river owing to the rebels on the banks firing into our boats, and the consequent delay of the marine fleet to land troops to chase them away.

We reached Fort Henry on the 28th and lay until May, 1, when all those who were convalescent were landed at Fort Heiman under charge of a Lieutenant of the Eighty-sixth Illinois, whose name I have forgotten, and who, by a series of applications, finally succeeded in getting himself transferred to Paducah, leaving us in the care of Lieutenant Taylor, of the Third Minnesota.

The Third Minnesota and part of the Eleventh Illinois composed the post troops of Fort Heiman. Our detachment, consisting of convalescents from all the regiments in the Provisional Brigade and some from Dodge's Division was sent across the river to Fort Henry to guard the telegraph office.

Lieutenant Taylor was quite accommodating, procuring clothing, camp and garrison equipage in abundance, so that in a short time we were most comfortably fixed up in the old fort. About the 12th we were reinforced by a squad from Gallatin, under command of Sergeant Thomas W. Loving, of Company A, of our regiment, who were hunting the regiment.

In a few days the wires brought in the sad tidings of the death of Colonel Hathaway and the fate of the brigade.

On the 31st Fort Heiman's troops were ordered to Vicksburg and we were sent to Nashville via Fort Donelson.

After a march of twelve miles across the country we arrived at the latter place, reported to the Post Commander for transportation to Nashville, drew rations and took up our quarters in a hay shed near the levee. We waited here for boats until June 3rd, when we went on board the steamer "Emma" and ran up to Clarksville; the next morning moved over to the steamer "Goody Friends" and ran into Nashville about eight o'clock that night.

We reported to the Maxwell Barracks and were forwarded to Murfreesboro, reporting there to General

Rosecrans' headquarters.

The Fifty-first and Seventy-third were sent to General Crittenden's, thence to General Wood's, the Seventy-third, thence to Colonel Harker's, thence to Lieutenant-Colonel White beck's command, the Sixty-fifth Ohio V.I., where we were subdivided and assigned to the different companies of that regiment as so many recruits.

Here were collected the Seventy-third convalescents from all the convalescent camps and hospitals within the department since the capture of our regiment, also those sent back from East Port and Tuscumbia.

The company commanders seemed to look upon us as permanently transferred, adopting us on their reports and muster-rolls as gained by transfer. We should have preferred being with our own messmates and comrades at Indianapolis, where the enlisted men of our regiment had been sent and were then on duty, but complaining availed us nothing. We were in for a separate campaign to make up for our failure to accompany the regiment on the raid. Our officers were not released from prison and we must bide our time of detached service though it should prove unpleasant and irksome.

On the 20th of June Colonel Whitebeck gave Lieutenant Eaton, who had returned with the sick from Tuscumbia, permission to collect the scattered men and organize a separate company or detachment. We therefore were organized and took our position, the third in the left wing of the regiment, constituting the 11th or 73rd Company.

We represented every company in the regiment and mustered one First Lieutenant and one First Sergeant, two sergeants, three Corporals, and 42 Privates, making an aggregate of 51.

Our reports showed more men present than any other company, and of course we had a proportionate amount of duty to perform.

Thus organized and equipped with the necessary

shelter tents and other camp and garrison equipage needful for our comfort we marched out from Murfreesboro with the Army of the Cumberland early on the morning of the 24th.

We kept a southeasterly direction during the day, and the rain which set in during the morning continued to pour down upon us steadily. We were sent on picket on going into camp, and a soaking night we had of it in the dark, wet woods. We made but little progress the next two days, the rain still falling and the roads abounding in sticky mud.

On the 27th and 28th the sun shone down with intense heat between showers and we still made slow progress over muddy and mountainous roads.

Our division reached Manchester on the 30th and went into camp, only to break it again on the 1st of July and continue our march toward Hillsboro. Corporal Brumfield and W. E. Gorsuch, Company C, and Alexander Smith, Company I, were left sick at Manchester. Smith, we afterwards learned, never recovered, but soon was quietly sleeping the soldier's sleep that knows no waking.

We heard that Tullahoma was evacuated by the rebel army.

On the 2nd we marched to within a mile of Pelham, wading streams, and walked in mud during the whole day. Here we performed a series of countermarches between Pelham and Hillsboro, a continued re-wading of the numerous swollen streams on the road, the object of which movements I have never been able to learn.

On the 4th we went into camp near Pelham. It was another rainy day and our company celebrated the glorious anniversary by going out as guard to a forage train.

On the 6th, still raining. Rations scarce and getting scarcer, one ration being issued for three days.

Early on the morning of the 8th we were called out for undress parade to hear a dispatch from General Crittenden, telling us that Vicksburg had fallen, General Pemberton surrendering the whole of his command to General Grant on the 4th. Loud cheers going up from every camp in the, division, rent the air, accompanied by the sound of booming guns, proclaiming the glad tidings in echoes and re-echoes among the mountains miles around. The same day we marched back to Hillsboro and encamped, leaving General Wagner's brigade at Pelham.

The next day moved the camp to a very pleasant piece of wood near the famous Big Spring and fixed up summer quarters. Here we obtained blackberries, apples, potatoes and other vegetables in abundance, and a reasonble amount of meats, though it was mostly fresh beef.

Policing, drilling and guarding, with foraging for a variation, at once became our daily duty. Everything passed on tamely, no events of importance crowding themselves upon us.

On the 20th we received news of John Morgan's capture in Ohio, and it created a general good feeling through the camp. On the 29th, the Sixty-fifth were paid off, all but the Seventy-third Company, the Paymaster saying that he could not pay our detachment. We stood in the background, in sight, but not in possession, of the "Almighty greenback." The Sixty-fifth boys were kind and obliging, however, some of them offering to loan us money and wait for it until we might be paid.

About this time we saw a paragraph in the Cincinnati Commercial stating that General Rosecrans had issued an order for those detachments of the Fifty-first and Seventy-third Indiana on duty with the department to report to their regiments at Indianapolis. This was good news for us, but the order didn't come, and we consoled ourselves with the reflection that we were not prisoners of war, as our esteemed officers were. However hard the duty, under whatever circumstances, though they be unpleasant, yet we were out beneath Heaven's canopy of cloud, and free to breathe earth's purest air, and our situation was a happy one compared to languishing imprisonment.

Early on the morning of the 16th of August we broke our pleasant camp at Hillsboro and set out amid a shower of rain for Pelham. Lieutenant Eaton being sick, Lieutenant Smith, of Company G, Sixty-fifth, was assigned to our command during the march.

We camped near Pelham and resumed the march again at five o'clock the next morning. We made the ascent of the mountains by night with wagons taking only half their loads. The assistance of men with ropes was necessary to bring the wagons and artillery up the steep places. The task was an arduous one, and I remember seeing Colonel Harker, small as he was, with coat off and sleeves rolled up, pulling at the ropes like a grenadier, while our brigade teams were ascending.

On the 18th, train up with the second load and all repacked ready to proceed by noon. An issue of whiskey was the so-called reward for our hard labor as the teams were coming up the steep mountains all night long, and some were obliged to keep fires burning on each side of the road so that the rope hands might work effectively.

We marched on toward Tracy City, the Sixty-fifth bringing up the rear. We reached Tracy early the next morning, made coffee there, and then proceeded on our way. We saw several fearful looking specimens of the large mountain rattlesnake during this day's march.

On the 20th we made the descent of the mountains to Thurman in the beautiful Sequatchie Valley, East Tennessee. Here we found an excellent spring of water, vegetables in abundance, the best potatoes, peaches and apples it has ever been my good fortune to obtain in any part of the South. General Wood issued a congratulatory order to the troops, highly complimenting them for the heroism and soldierly manner in which they had performed the difficult march from Hillsboro.

A rest of two days and we began drilling again, having Brigade drill every afternoon. Our brigade consisted of four Regiments, the Sixty-fourth, Sixty-fifth, and One hundred and twenty-fifth Ohio V.I., and the Third Kentucky V.I., with the Sixth Ohio V. Battery.

General Wood was anxious to get the Fifty-first and the Seventy-third Indiana back in his division, and on that account, we believed, wished to keep our detachments with him, thinking they might assist in bringing about that result. We were fully satisfied that he already had the order from

General Crittenden to return us to Nashville to join our regiment.

At last the expected order came late in the afternoon of the 30th. Captain Haley, of the Fifty-first, had received the order from Rosecrans, unknown to General Wood, and he was therefore obliged to let us return. We were to report to Captain Haley early the next morning and go with the supply train to Tracy City.

That night we closed up our relationship with the Sixty-fifth, disposed of what camp and garrison equipage we could, turned over a few guns to the regiment, drew three days' rations, and were all ready to leave the camp at daylight of the 31st. Upon going to Colonel Whitebeck, after receiving marching orders to get his order for rations, he was very kind and complimentary indeed. He said he was glad we were to return to our own regiment, but sorry to see us go.

That we had been good soldiers while with him, kept up the good name of our regiment in the brigade, and he would send us away with full haversacks, giving us three days' full rations, when he was only issuing half rations to the regiment.

Early the next morning we bid a final adieu to the Sixty-fifth, with a much better opinion of it than when we entered it at Murfreesboro. We left some friends with whom we regretted to part, among them Major Brown, than whom a kinder man, in camp or on the march, never wore golden leaves.

There are some other minor incidents connected with our stay with the Sixty- fifth which might be remembered with interest by the detachment, but which I shall not here narrate. How certain petitions were circulated while at Hillsboro ..., what we thought when leaving the camp with Lieutenant Eaton sick..., and how two rear guards that day failed to make camp at night... How on the mountain we laid in the woods all one damp, chilly night..., and how noisy the regiment was with the continual cry of "All over," and other similar phrases.

We reported to Captain Haley at the foot of the

mountain, and after a full day's ride in the "hard trotting" government wagons we reached Tracy City. After eating our suppers we spread down our blankets on the green sod and enjoyed a good night's repose.

There was but an engine and one car at the station, and next morning, huddled together on this limited train, we came down the mountains to Cowan, on the Nashville and Chattanooga railroad. The ride reminded one of sliding downhill on a handsled in dim distant days of boyhood. It was so steep, so winding, so novel and picturesque. This road was built expressly for bringing coal from the mines at Tracy City, and none but peculiar engines and cars were serviceable on it.

Changing cars at Cowan, we continued our ride until night found us in Nashville, putting up at the Maxwell barracks.

September 2nd. Up to this time we made sure of being sent to Indianapolis, and, once there, sure of furloughs home; but General Granger, commanding post, had use for us in Nashville, so our railroad riding stopped for a while.

We relieved detachments of the Third Ohio and Eightieth Illinois stationed at the siege guns about the city and at Fort Johnson, and entered immediately upon our new duties. We found the drill upon the heavy guns to be simple, and after getting fixed up, comfortably we thought the heavy artillery after all was the "right arm" of the service. Not in the sense of being the most destructive to the enemy, for I have serious doubts about our projectiles going to the intended place, if Nashville had been attacked at this time. We never had permission to fire at a target, and our knowledge, therefore, was all theoretical.

On the 10th received news of the occupation of Chattanooga and Cumberland Gap by our troops, which good tidings were celebrated at night by an enthusiastic meeting at the statehouse.

On the 21st came the rumors of severe fighting, which proved to be the battle of Chickamagua. Fearful slaughter and almost a defeat, a tolerable price for the stronghold of Chattanooga.

About this time our friend and comrade, Sergeant Thomas W. Loving, of Company A, was sent to the hospital, where he died after an illness of a few days. He was buried in the city cemetery, and a headboard there tells his name and the number of his grave, 5,266.

October 3rd. Visited the officers' hospital and saw Colonel Whitebeck, Lieutenant Hinman, Lieutenant Gardner, and other officers of the Sixty-fifth Ohio who were wounded at Chickamagua. Heard with sorrow that Major Brown had fallen on that sanguinary field, and many more of the regiment found a final resting place beneath the soil for which they died stubbornly contesting.

On the 25th the Seventy-third came to Nashville, arriving about nine o'clock at night, put up at the Maxwell barracks, and went into camp by the pike, near the penitentiary the next day. The Fifty-first encamped with them, and both regiments went on miscellaneous duty as post troops.

November 6, Captain Haley, commanding heavy artillery, was relieved and ordered to his regiment which anticipated marching orders soon for Chattanooga.

On the 10th Lieutenant Eaton was also relieved and returned to his regiment. On the 12th, Captain Williamson, commanding the Seventy-third, was ordered to report to Captain White, Post Chief of Artillery, with his command, for duty on artillery, and on the 13th, nearly five months from the day of its organization, our detachment was broken up, the members all returning to their respective companies.

Thus melted away the Seventy-third Company into the Seventy-third Regiment again, in the aggregate present of which it has ever since figured. Eventless and tame as this sketch may be, I trust it will not be entirely void of interest to those conversant with the subject, and that it may form subject matter for a parenthetical chapter in the history of our regiment.

Following is the complete roll of the Seventy-third Company, known in the Sixty-fifth Ohio as Company "Q."

Company A - Henry W. Gilbert, Horace F. Gordonier, Peter Johann, Lloyd Lamphier, Philip Litter, Sergeant Thomas W. Loving, George Metz, John Tanner.

Company B - Oriss Bentley, Ephraim C. Cornelius, Lorenzo P. Fields, Minor S. Marble, Christian Phillipi, George W. Shippy, Benjamin S. White, Fred Whit brook.

Company C - Joseph Bivins, Corporal Stanton J. Brumfield, Egbert Finney, Wilber E. Gorsuch.

Company D - James E. Clem, Thomas Gilson.

Company E - Lewis Brown, Richard Gibbons, John Maudlin, Ethan A. Murray, John M. Murray, Charles Shutts.

Company F - Leander W. Crumb, Andrew Jacobs, William H. Lloyd, Jacob Maxey, John W. Patterson, Corporal George T. Poulson.

Company G - William H. Downs, William C. Searight, William H. H. Smith.

Company H - Sergeant George B. Custer, Henry H. Glidden, Daniel Haworth, James Hensley, James Kearns, John Murphy.

Company I - Lieutenant William C. Eaton, Robert Flewellyn, Eli J. Gordon, Corporal Uriah D. Jaqua, Alexander Smith, Delarma Webb.

Company K - 1st Sergeant Job Barnard, Robert Behan, Michael McAuliffe, Hiram W. Miller.

Chapter Eight

RETURN OF REGIMENT TO TENNESSEE

After the return of the regiment to Nashville, on the 25th of October, 1863, some of the men continued on duty in charge of the siege guns, and others returned to the regiment for such general duty as was given it, until the 12th of November, when the regiment, then in command of Captain Williamson, of Company I, was ordered to report to Captain White, Chief of Artillery, when for a time the whole regiment was doing duty in the artillery service.

On the 12th of January, 1864, in obedience to an order received on the 9th, a detail of one man from each company started home on recruiting service for the regiment. This detail was as follows:

Company A, Henry W. Gilbert;
Company B, Sergeant L. T. Penwell;
Company C, 1st Sergeant G. L. Pearson;
Company D, Corporal William H. H. Simons;
Company E, 1st Sergeant Charles W. Wheeler;
Company F, Leander W. Crumb;
Company G. 1st Sergeant Alexander Wilson;
Company H, Private Henry H. Glidden,
Company I, Lieutenant William C. Eaton;
Company K, 1st Sergeant Job Barnard.

Major Wade was exchanged, and reached Nashville on March 27th, 1864, finding Captain Williamson still in command of the regiment, with headquarters on the corner of Broad and Vine Streets, but the regiment was scattered around in various places in the vicinity of Nashville; some of the men at Fort Negley, some on the Northwestern Railroad, some at Cheatham's Mills, twenty-two miles from the city, getting out timber for stockades, bridges, etc., and some still engaged in charge of the siege guns about the city, and the recruiting party just mentioned still in Indiana.

The regiment was then attached to the Twelfth Army Corps, Third Division, First Brigade, Army of the Tennessee.

Major Wade began at once to get the scattered fragments of the regiment together, and by April 3rd moved the camp down one mile in rear of Fort Gillem, and on April 9th had sufficient of the men together to have the first dress parade, and on the next day had battalion drill.

The first general order of the regiment seems to have been issued on April 10th, as follows:

"The following shall be the order in camp: Reveille at daybreak, breakfast call 6 a.m., sick call 7:30, guard-mount 8:30, officer's recitation 9 o'clock, company drill 10 o'clock, recall 11 o'clock, dinner 12 noon, police 1 p.m., battalion drill 3 p.m., dress parade 5 o'clock, retreat call 6, supper 6:30, tattoo 8:30, taps 9 p.m. By order of A. B. Wade, Major commanding."

A number of men were still on detached duty, but on April 14 some from Fort Negley returned to the regiment, and permission was given by General Rosecrans to move camp to Lavergne.

On April 19, Major Wade, accompanied by Captain Boyd, of Company F, made an inspection tour of Posts Nos. 5, 6, and 7, occupied by portions of our regiment, the ride being about 25 miles.

On April 28th, while still in camp at Lavergne, Major Wade, with seven mounted men, and a Union citizen as guide, made a scout through Rutherford, Davidson, and Williamson counties, for Green Hall, Bob Battle, and Everett Patterson, noted guerillas of that neighborhood. The party had a skirmish or two with the enemy, but they made their escape.

On April 30th Lieutenant Hagenbuck, of Company D, was detailed by Major Wade as Provost Marshal, and Lieutenant Hubbard, of Company H, was detailed as Post

Commissary.

On May 19th Company K arrived at Lavergne from Cheatham's Mills, and Company D from Fort Negley, and the usual drilling and camp duties, with an occasional scouting party, continued until June 6th, when Lieutenant-Colonel Walker, having been exchanged and released from prison, returned to the regiment and took command.

On June 8th Major Wade went to Nashville and brought down two trains, on which Lieutenant-Colonel Walker, with seven of the companies, embarked for the south, leaving Major Wade with the other three companies to follow as soon as transportation could be procured.

On the 9th the rest of the regiment left Lavergne and went to Stevenson, Ala., where they transferred to the Memphis and Charleston railroad and went to Decatur Junction, Ala. There Lieutenant-Colonel Walker joined the companies under Major Wade, and the whole regiment being together once more, marched to Mooresville, a distance of four miles, where we remained until the 14th, when Colonel Walker, with companies D, E, F, H, I and K marched on to Triana, on the Tennessee River, relieving the Sixty-third Illinois Infantry at that place.

Major Wade, with companies A, B, C, and G went to the mouth of Limestone Creek. The duties of the regiment now were to guard the ferries and possible crossings of the river.

Major Wade, at Limestone, at once set to work making temporary fortifications. Substantial blockhouses were commenced and pushed to completion, small blockhouses were built at given points along the river, and the command distributed to occupy the same.

The "Johnnies" sometimes showed themselves on the opposite side of the river, and some communication was held with them under flag of truce.

June 18 Captain Eaton took Companies I and E and went down to Decatur Junction to guard the railroad, leaving only four companies at Triana.

Lieutenant Williams returned to the regiment from Libby Prison, after escaping with Colonel Streight, and others, through the tunnel, on April 2nd, and for a time took command of his company, but later was assigned to command Company H.

After we reached Triana he was detailed to command the patrol line along the river, having several mounted men and a squad of pioneers engaged in building stockades under his direction.

June 24 Lieutenant Reynolds returned to the regiment with convalescents from Lavergne, and assumed command of Company K for a short time. He resigned because of ill health and imprisonment, and from wounds received at Stone River, and left for home July 30.

That portion of the regiment on duty at Triana arranged to celebrate the 4th of July, and did so by raising a liberty pole on the regimental parade ground, and marched to the grove in the afternoon, where the Declaration of Independence was read and an oration delivered by C. F. Kimball, our Commissary Sergeant. Several patriotic toasts and responses were given, after which the meeting was dismissed by benediction from the Chaplain, and we all marched back to quarters, the regimental band playing "Yankee Doodle."

On July 10th Lieutenant-Colonel Walker received notice of the acceptance of his resignation, because of ill health, and greatly to the regret of the soldiers he left us for home on July 11th, when Major Wade came to Triana, and assumed command of the regiment. The officers signed resolutions, couched in strong and fitting words, expressive of their feelings at the loss of Colonel Walker, and on the 12th and 13th the non-commissioned officers and privates of the regiment passed resolutions of regret at the Lieutenant-Colonel's resignation and of deep loss felt by them in the death of Colonel Hathaway.

Companies G and C from Limestone came back to headquarters at Triana on the 13th.

July 22nd guerillas captured and burned a train filled with cotton near Huntsville, the smoke of which could be plainly seen from Triana.

On July 29th, Major Wade, with detachments from C, D, H, and G, numbering fifty men, crossed the river in rowboats at Watkin's Ferry and made a bold and rapid march to Summerville, a distance of nine miles. They captured ten horses and mules and a few rifles and shotguns found at private residences, and came back to camp about 5 p.m. The heat was severe.

On August 2nd, Captain Boyd, of Company F, and Lieutenant Grimes, of Company D, having resigned, took final leave of the regiment.

August 6th a six-pound gun with caisson, for which requisition had been made, was received and put in a commanding position at the ferry, and eight men were detailed from the regiment as gunners.

On August 15th a detail composed of about 103 crossed the river on a flat boat and a pontoon, making several trips across, and marched to Valhermosa Springs, some twelve miles from the river, where saltpetre works operated by the enemy were found, and the kettles destroyed and buildings burned. We took several horses and mules, saw three or four rebels, some of whom were captured, and we returned to camp in the afternoon almost exhausted from the severe heat and long march.

On August 31st the troops at Triana left for Decatur Junction, where the companies then engaged in guarding the road east of that point joined the regiment. The men from Triana did not arrive at the Junction until about 12 o'clock midnight.

On the morning of September 1st we left the Junction on a train of flat cars for Elk River Bridge, Nashville and Decatur Railroad. We learned that the purpose of our sudden march and expedition was to repel General Wheeler and his men, who, were threatening the railroad in that vicinity.

On September 2nd we remained all day in the hot sun on the side hill, where General Starkweather and his staff called to see us.

At night, after we had got comfortably fixed for sleeping, we were ordered to Prospect Hill to repair the fort, and we lay in the fort in the hot sun on the 3rd, 4th and 5th, many of the men being sick with chills and fever. A number were sent to the hospital at Pulaski and some sent back to Decatur.

On the 15th of September the regiment returned to Decatur Junction and thence to Mooresville, while Company K returned to the Piney Creeks, where it had been previously located, it and Company F having gone to the railroad from Triana under special orders of August 23rd, to relieve Companies A, E, and I, Company F being located at Limestone Creek Bridge and Little Limestone Bridge, and Company K at Big Piney Creek and Little Piney Creek.

At this time Major Wade received his commission as Lieutenant-Colonel, and on the 19th of September, in company with other officers who had also been promoted, went to Nashville to be mustered in.

They returned to the regiment on the 21st, and during their absence Company B was ordered back to Triana to garrison that place.

On September 24 heavy cannonading was heard in the direction of Athens, and at noon orders were received for the Seventy-third to march immediately for Decatur. The march began at 2 o'clock p.m., over bad roads full of mud, and we went into camp about 5 o'clock at Decatur.

Colonel Given, of the One hundred and second Ohio, was in command of the post. Part of his regiment and part of the Eighteenth Michigan and some United States colored troops were captured at Athens, and an attack on Decatur was anticipated.

On September 26th Colonel Doolittle, of the Eighteenth Michigan, took command.

Chapter Nine

BATTLE WITH BUFORD AT ATHENS

On the evening of the 28th of September, 1864, Lieutenant-Colonel Wade was ordered to proceed with his regiment to Athens and to retake that place, which had been captured by Forrest. Only five companies of the regiment were present at Decatur, the other companies remaining on detached duty on the line of the M. and C. Railroad and on the river, so that the force under command of Colonel Wade consisted of a portion of the Seventy-third, and 200 of the Tenth Indiana Cavalry.

They crossed the river at Decatur on a pontoon bridge, and boarded flat cars and started for Athens, fifteen miles distant, reaching the vicinity of the town about one o'clock at night, where they disembarked and went into camp, finding the track torn up at that point.

At daylight on the 29th the command moved forward cautiously and marched to the fort on the hill west from the station. They found the barracks inside the fort all burned, the chimneys only remaining. The fort was surrounded by a wide, deep ditch, the dirt from which had been thrown on the inside, forming a solid raised embankment. Abatis was placed around the outside of the ditch, rendering access more difficult, but there was no bomb-proof or shelter inside the fort to protect the garrison. It was feared that Forrest would return by way of Athens, that being the most direct route to the Mussel Shoals, where he could cross the river.

General Granger sent up to the support of Colonel Wade two rifled guns and 30 artillerymen of the First Tennessee Battery, and 200 men of the Second Tennessee Cavalry, with the Seventy-third baggage train with garrison and camp equipage.

September 29th reveille was sounded before daybreak, and the command formed in line to be ready should an early attack be made.

The following is taken verbatim from Colonel Wade's diary, giving his account of the building of a bomb-proof at this fort and the result of the fight.

"This splendid fort had been built with a great deal of trouble and expense, but the fatal mistake was made of not building a bomb-proof.

A happy thought finally struck me. I had not the time to build one inside the fort, and whatever was to be done must be done quickly, as I had no definite information in regard to the enemy, and was liable to be attacked at any moment.

The outside ditch would serve my purpose admirably, and I immediately set to work a force of men and all the teams available in hauling up logs from the old huts in the vicinity. These laid across the ditch makes it perfectly bomb-proof, as any shot striking it will do so slantingly, and must therefore glance off. An entrance into this novel arrangement will be effected by a passageway dug under the gate of the fort.

If Forrest gives me until tomorrow noon I will fight his command, artillery and all.

There are about 100 wounded here. One dead negro soldier was found upon the battlefield today and buried. A hard rain storm is now setting in."

"October 1st, 1864. I was heartily glad to see my wagon train come in this noon. Huntsville was attacked last night, and Major McBath, with the Second Tennessee Cavalry, had been ordered at midnight to proceed to that place, and started this morning at daybreak, but came tearing back this afternoon; having met the enemy's advance guard four miles from Huntsville coming this way.

At 3 p.m. the pickets on the Huntsville road were driven in, and at the same time a drenching rain storm commenced.

I deployed one company of dismounted cavalry to engage the enemy, who had taken position behind the railroad, and commenced moving the baggage into the fort.

Firing was kept up briskly on the skirmish line until dusk, when I reinforced it with Company G of the Seventy-third to prevent the rebels from gaining possession of a cluster of houses near the fort.

The cavalry dismounted, fastened their horses, and were stationed inside of the fort.

The passageway under the gate leading into my bomb-proof was but a foot deep when skirmishing first commenced, but I put all the men on to it that could work, with instructions to dig away, no matter how hard the fighting, and by midnight it was large enough to be used.

My garrison now consisted of five companies of the Seventy-third Indiana Infantry, under command of Captain Eaton; four companies of the Second Tennessee Cavalry, under Major McBath; two companies of the Tenth Indiana Dismounted Cavalry, commanded by Captain Gaffney; and a section of the Second Tennessee Artillery, Battery A, under Lieutenant Tobin, in all, about 500 effective men, opposed to which was Brigadier-General A. Buford's Division of Cavalry and a battery of four guns, numbering 4,000 men. His advantage was in numbers. Ours was in fortifications, a good bomb-proof, and a better cause.

During the night the noise made by the enemy's guns enabled me to locate their position exactly, and the two pieces in the fort were brought to bear upon them, ready to answer their fire as soon as opened. Three companies were moved into the bombproof, the balance placed in advantageous positions, and we were ready to fight Buford and his whole command.

October 2nd, 1864. Half an hour before daybreak the

men were aroused and stood to arms. From early daylight till 6 a.m. a brisk fire was kept up with small-arms, principally from the west side, where a thick growth of timber approached to within short range of the fort.

At 6 a.m. the enemy opened with one gun situated southwest from the fort on the Brown's Ferry road, which was promptly responded to.

Ten minutes after, three rifled pieces opened fire upon us in quick succession from a slight elevation one-half mile north. With such a cross fire there was scarcely a spot in the fort but what could be reached by a shell, and I immediately moved the troops into the bomb-proof, leaving a sufficient number as sentinels to watch for indications of an assault.

I had previously given orders to Lieutenant Arnold, commanding Company E, to halt any flag of truce that might approach, some distance from the fort in order that they might not discover our bomb-proof.

After half an hour's practice the enemy's guns obtained the range and threw shells into the fort with great accuracy. I had planted the regimental flag of the Seventy-third on the parapet, and it suffered considerably, two shells passing through and tearing great holes.

A caisson cover was torn off and set on fire within a few inches of the ammunition. Private A. H. Kersey, of Company I, instantly put it out with a pail of water at the imminent risk of being blown to atoms. A tall chimney was tumbled to the ground, hardly leaving one brick upon another. Thirty horses were killed or wounded which were fastened a few yards from the walls of the fort. Five shells struck exactly at the position where Company D of the Seventy-third had stood.

About sixty rounds were fired at us. Twenty-two struck the fort, nearly all inside, the balance bursting overhead or passing beyond. Our two guns returned this severe fire cooly and steadily. Had we remained silent the rebs would not have wasted so much ammunition upon us.

At eight o'clock General Buford, concluding that we must be pretty well demoralized, ceased firing, and we soon saw a horseman approaching with a flag of truce. I delegated Captain William C. Eaton, of Company I, to meet him and try to ascertain the disposition of their troops while I was answering whatever communication should be sent.

While the flag was approaching I had leisure to examine the field with a glass, and soon discovered they were moving up a dismounted line in front of my weakest point. This was a violation of the flag, but I concluded not to notice it and simply ordered out three companies and trained the artillery upon their line, which was moved up within 200 yards of the fort. Private Johnson, who had accompanied the Captain, soon brought in a sealed envelope which contained the following:

"Headquarters in the Field, Near Athens, Ala., October 2, 1864. Commanding Officer, U. S. Forces, Athens, Ala.

Sir: Having invested your place with a sufficient force to reduce it in a short time, for the sake of humanity, I demand the surrender of the fort, garrison, etc. Certain conditions will attend the surrender, with which conditions the bearer of this will acquaint you.

I am, sir, with much respect, etc.

A. BUFORD, Brig. Genl. P.A.C.S., Comdg."

Buford's Adjutant, General Small, proved to be the bearer. I had some curiosity to know what conditions he would offer, but as that might lead him to think that we would surrender if they were liberal enough, I sat down on a cracker box and wrote the following:

"Headquarters United States Forces, Athens, Ala., October 2, 1864. Brigadier-General A. Buford, Commanding Confederate Forces, In front of Athens, Ala.

Sir: I have the honor to acknowledge the receipt of your communication of this date, demanding the surrender of the fort and garrison under my command. In answer I would say that having a sufficient force to defend the place I decline to surrender.
Very respectfully, your obedient servant,
A. B. WADE, Lieutenant-Colonel Seventy-third Indiana Comdg."

And sending it out ordered the flag off and Captain Eaton to return immediately. It seems the cowardly rebels had basely taken advantage of this flag, and while I was engaged writing an answer stole six wagons and four ambulances directly from under my guns. I did not know this at the time, but because they had changed position under the flag I determined to teach them a lesson, and as soon as the flag disappeared ordered four companies and the artillery to open on their new line. They fell back in confusion, leaving four dead.
They continued to annoy us with their sharpshooters, who had taken possession of headquarters. I finally ordered eight shell to be sent through the building, which drove them out in a hurry. I then sent skirmishers out in every direction at 10 a.m., suspecting that Buford had found a harder nut to crack than he anticipated, and was leaving, which proved to be true., The cavalry immediately pursued, and found that they had retreated down the Florence road. Our loss was only two slightly wounded. That of the enemy unknown, as he carried off all his wounded. This victory of ours has a great significance from the fact that a larger garrison surrendered this same fort when in better condition only a week or two since.
I estimate the saving on casualties by our bombproof to be at least 50, as shells cannot explode in a small fort filled with men without killing somebody."

Chapter Ten

EVACUATION OF ATHENS AND SKIRMISHING WITH HOOD AT DECATUR

After General Buford's retreat from Athens the troops remained there under command of Colonel Wade until October 4th, when the Second Tennessee Cavalry left us and 150 men of the One hundred and second Ohio and one other company of the Seventy- third Indiana were added to the garrison.

Lieutenant L. P. Williams, of Company K, who had gone to Athens from Decatur just prior to the fight, remained there, and was appointed Post Commissary.

The command continued to increase in numbers until, on the 6th of October, there were six companies of the Seventy-third, 316 men, Captain Eaton commanding; 170 men of the One hundred and second Ohio, Captain Beerbower commanding; 116 dismounted men of the Tenth Indiana Cavalry, Captain Gaffney commanding; 237 men of the One hundred and twenty-fifth Illinois Infantry, Captain Cook commanding; 31 men of the First Tennessee Artillery Battery, Lieutenant Tobin commanding; - a total of some 870 men fit for duty, besides about 200 sick and wounded.

On the 7th the men of the One hundred and second Ohio were ordered to Decatur. Two more dead rebels were found in the brush, killed in the battle of the 2nd.

On October 13th Company K returned to the regiment from the Piney Creeks, and about 300 men of the Ninth Ohio Cavalry were added to the garrison.

On October 27th Lieutenant-Colonel Wade was ordered to Decatur with his regiment, leaving one Company - C, and the convalescents at Athens, with Lieutenant Williams in command.

The rebel, General Hood, was threatening Decatur, and fighting had already commenced. The detachment arrived about two o'clock in the morning of the 28th, with 150 men available for duty.

A portion of the Seventy-third had arrived at the fort the day preceding Colonel Wade's arrival, and had made a charge, re-establishing the picket lines, which had been driven back by the charge from the rebels.

At daylight on the 28th it was discovered that the enemy had fortified their new lines, which extended from the river above the fort to the river below, a distance of about three miles.

One company of the Eighteenth Michigan moved out on the right of the Seventy-third, flanked the enemy's line, and charged down upon them with a yell which surprised the rebel line and broke it to the rear without firing a shot. The artillery from our fort immediately opened on them with telling effect, killing and wounding a number, while about 100 were taken prisoners. The enemy immediately advanced another line, and the Seventy-third was ordered out to cover the retreat of the Eighteenth Michigan

We double-quicked to the southeast sallyport and pushed out under a heavy skirmish fire. We deployed to the right and left, and lay down to escape the fire of the enemy, and after remaining there some time firing and being fired upon, we returned to the fort without the loss of a man, although two were wounded.

One man was killed in the charge made on the 27th, Robert Flewellyn, of Company I.

In the afternoon of the 28th we were sent out to hold the extreme left rifle pits. The enemy were in considerable force in our front and a lively skirmish was kept up all the afternoon. Eighty rounds of ammunition to the man was thus expended by us with but small results, as both sides were well protected.

A regiment of colored troops, under Colonel Morgan,

was sent out to charge a rebel battery on our left, but the position was too strong and they fell back with a loss of 40 killed and wounded.

In the evening we were relieved from the picket line and returned to the fort.

On the 29th we still remained on picket duty, but the enemy seemed to be leaving, and soon our skirmishers occupied their ground and we recovered the body of Robert Flewellyn, and also found several of their own men left unburied in their "gopher holes."

On the 30th it was assumed that Hood's whole army was crossing the river at Florence, and it was thought that we would march immediately toward Nashville by way of Athens, and our regiment was ordered back to Athens, where we arrived and found everything all right.

On October 31st we had positive orders about four o'clock in the afternoon to evacuate Athens at once, without waiting for railroad transportation. The Seventy-third remained, however, until night, and then marched to Decatur Junction.

Considerable government property was ordered to be destroyed; and it was hastily set on fire and destroyed.

The next morning we were ordered to return to Athens, and we marched back, arriving there about 3 p.m. The hasty evacuation had evidently been a mistake, either of the General Commanding, or a misunderstanding on the part of Colonel O'Dowd, of the One hundred and eighty-first Ohio, who had, as ranking officer, command of the place on our return there on the 30th.

On November 7th orders were received from General Granger to be ready to evacuate whenever the enemy should appear in force. Colonel Wade telegraphed for permission to remain, claiming that he could hold the post against ten times our number, but received the reply that the order was from General Thomas, and was imperative.

Accordingly, we set off our baggage on the cars.

On November 4th it was apprehended that Decatur was to be again attacked, and 100 men from our regiment, under command of Lieutenant Clark, went down to Decatur and remained in the trenches all night.

Next day we moved to the hotel porch at the close of a rainy day, and some of us slept inside the hotel on the night of the 16th, but on the 17th we returned to Athens on a special train and found our baggage all returned.

On November 18th Colonel Wade received an order from General Granger, assigning him to the command of all that part of the Tennessee and Alabama and M. and C Railroads, then under command of Brigadier General Starkweather, extending from Athens to Hurricane Creek.

On November 19th Captain Gaffney's company of the Tenth Indiana Cavalry was added to our forces for courier duty.

On November 23rd Colonel Wade, Lieutenant Williams, and some of the scouts escorted the Paymaster in his visit to pay off the companies on the railroad and at Triana, and late in the afternoon of that day we received orders to evacuate Athens again.

Lieutenant Hagenbuck had been left in command of the regiment, and on the 24th, under his command, we vacated Athens for the last time and set out on our march to Decatur Junction, where we went into camp, Colonel Wade having met us on the march there.

Chapter Eleven

EVACUATION AND REOCCUPANCY OF NORTHERN ALABAMA

On November 25th we marched to Huntsville, going by way of Mooresville. We called in the companies located on the railroad and at Triana as we marched along, and when we reached Huntsville about 10:30 o'clock at night found the troops preparing to evacuate.

We lay in camp all day the 26th, amidst great excitement. Business men were trying to dispose of their goods in order to get away. Colored people and white refugees were making preparations to leave; also many were going off on top of the trains, and some old buildings were set on fire, without orders, which kept the town lighted up at night. The whole regiment was placed on patrol duty.

On the 27th we broke camp about eleven o'clock and started on the march toward Stevenson, and we marched out about eight miles. There was a large number of refugees and negroes following us with their household goods and bundles, many of them carrying them on their heads.

On the 28th we continued our march and crossed Paint Rock River and went into camp nearby. Our baggage wagons failed to reach us.

On the 29th we marched on to Larkinsville and encamped, at which place our teams came up.

On the 30th marched on to Bellefonte, the Seventy-third in advance all day. The roads were bad and had to be repaired in many places by our pioneer squad in order for us to get over. About 60 of the Seventy- third were mounted and were under command of Lieutenant Williams.

On December 1st we marched to within three miles of Stevenson, where we went into camp, the refugees and negroes camping on all sides of us. It was estimated that there were about 3,000 of these followers in camp that night.

On December 2nd we marched into Stevenson, on the railroad, and the wagons were brought in on the cars.

We went into camp near the large spring, and found a German regiment, the Fifty-eighth New York, whose Colonel was in command of the post.

On the 3rd our teams were brought in, and on the 4th General Granger arrived and assumed command of the post. Lieutenant-Colonel Wade was placed in command of the "Redoubt Harker." The redoubt mounted six guns and was provided with a good stockade inside. The telegraph was cut and the railroad torn up between Stevenson and Nashville.

Most of the regiment remained at Stevenson until December 19th. The weather was wet and cold most of the time, and the men were occupied in picket duty, building and repairing quarters, and fortifying the place against an anticipated attack.

On the 14th a detail of 30 men, including Company K, under command of Lieutenant Williams, was sent to the bridge across Paint Rock River. Thirty men from the One hundred and second Ohio, under command of Captain Benton Beerbower, were also sent, and the whole detachment was under the command of Captain Beerbower.

This detail arrived at Paint Rock on the 15th, and on the 16th and 17th they heard cannonading in the direction of Nashville.

On the 18th news came to the regiment in Stevenson of the battle of Nashville, in which General Thomas had defeated General Hood, and on the 19th orders were received to occupy again Northern Alabama.

Colonel William P. Lyon, of the Thirteenth Wisconsin, who was commanding the brigade, was ordered to Huntsville with his regiment, and Lieutenant- Colonel Wade was given command of the brigade. This resulted in placing the Seventy-third in command of Captain James M. Beeber of

Company D until after we reached Huntsville.

Marching orders having been received, the brigade moved out to the Tennessee River at Caperton's Landing and camped. After much difficulty because of the bad roads and mud, the brigade was finally loaded on the gunboats "Chattanooga" and "Stone River," which moved down the river, anchoring at Bellefonte, Ala.

On the morning of the 21st the fleet moved on to Limestone Point, and there a council of war was held, General Granger finally deciding that the boats should return to Whiting instead of attempting to make an attack on Decatur, and on December 23d all the troops disembarked at Whiting, and went into camp, and in the evening of that day orders were received for the command to hasten to Huntsville, anticipating that General Forrest was approaching that place. The distance was about ten miles, and Huntsville was reached about 10 o'clock p.m., the brigade marching in the following order: the Eighteenth Michigan, Seventy- third Indiana, 29th Indiana, and One hundred and second Ohio.

On December 24th it turned out that the anticipated attack of Forrest was an error, and General Steadman's troops came in on the trains with about 9,000 men, and at one o'clock of that day our brigade was ordered back to Whiting, except our regiment, which was ordered to remain at Huntsville, much to the satisfaction of the men.

The detachment of the Seventy-third Indiana and One hundred and second Ohio at Paint Rock Bridge were ordered to Huntsville, and arrived on December 21st.

Christmas Day was celebrated in camp at Huntsville.

On December 31st, Lieutenant-Colonel Wade was ordered to Brownsboro with 150 men; 100 remained at Brownsboro, and 50 were sent to Hurricane Creek. Orders soon came for the 100 men at Brownsboro to go on to Paint Rock, and this detachment reached Paint Rock about daybreak on New Year's Day, January 1st, 1865, and found the place evacuated by the enemy and took peaceable possession.

The headquarters of the regiment remained in Huntsville until January 13th, when we left camp at eight o'clock in the morning and took the train for Larkinsville, reaching there about sundown.

On the 14th Company K began work building a log cabin, supposed to be strong enough for a stockade, and when about finished on the 20th the company was ordered to Paint Rock Station, or Camden, under command of 1st Sergeant Barnard, and Lieutenant Williams was ordered to Officers' Hospital at Nashville for treatment.

The headquarters of the regiment remaining at Larkinsville, Colonel Wade appointed Lieutenant R. M. Brown, of Company D, Provost Marshal, and Lieutenant W. S. Ramsey, of the same company, Commissary.

On the 10th Colonel Lyon visited the camp and inspected the blockhouse and authorized Colonel Wade to build according to his own plans.

Company E was sent to Woodville Station to garrison that place.

On the 28th Colonel Wade was placed in command of the railroad defenses as far as Stevenson.

On January 30th Lieutenant Thomas, of Company C, returned to the regiment from imprisonment, having been confined since his capture in May, 1863. He assumed command of Company C, and Lieutenant Slick was appointed Assistant Commissary of Subsistence.

On February 2nd, Lieutenant Brown, of Company E, returned from his long imprisonment and joined his company at Woodville.

On February 5th we received a six-pound gun and caisson from Battery D, First Missouri.

On the 7th Abram Finney, of Company C, while on picket, accidentally shot himself, and died in a few minutes.

Skirmishing occurred with the guerillas at various points along the line of the road, 150 guerillas camping within five miles of Larkinsville.

February 17 Company H and the pioneers at Gurley's tank, while out foraging, were attacked by a company of the Fourth Alabama Cavalry, the fight continuing about half an hour, one man killed on the side of the enemy and one wounded and brought into camp. Our boys sustained no loss.

An attack was made on Woodville, and one wagon from Company E was captured. The order was issued by Colonel Wade to the effect that if the citizens did not prevent the guerilla outrages going on in the country he should be obliged to burn their houses.

On February 22nd Washington's birthday was celebrated, the celebration being enlivened by the news of the surrender of Charleston, S. C., and the hoisting of the stars and stripes again over Fort Sumpter.

On March 1st Colonel Wade promoted Albert H. Kersey, of Company I, to the position of Corporal as a recognition of his bravery at Athens in extinguishing the burning caisson at the peril of his life.

At this time the various companies of the regiment were located and commanded as follows:

Company A, Stevens Gap, Lieutenant George S. Clark commanding.
Company B, Larkinsville, Lieutenant J. H. Kiersted commanding.
Company C, Larkinsville, Lieutenant Alexander N. Thomas commanding.
Company D, Paint Rock, Captain James M. Beeber commanding.
Company E, Woodville Tank, Lieutenant John L. Brown commanding.
Company F, Larkinsville, Lieutenant Otto H. Sollan commanding.
Company G, Hurricane Creek, Lieutenant Alexander Wilson

commanding.
Company H, Gurley's Tank, Lieutenant Wilson Dailey commanding.
Company I, Larkinsville, Captain William C. Eaton commanding.
Company K, Camden Station, 1st Sergeant Job Barnard commanding.

    Colonel Wade had command of the whole line of railroad from Huntsville to Stevenson, a distance of 60 miles, and in addition to the Seventy-third had detachments from the following regiments: One hundred and first, One hundred and sixth, One hundred and tenth, and One hundred and eleventh United States Colored Infantry, the Eighteenth Michigan Pioneers, and One hundred and second Ohio, and three companies of the Alabama Cavalry acting as scouts. Lieutenant Uptigrove was appointed A.A.G.
    On March 22nd the enemy appeared in several places along our line. They met six members of Company C and wounded two of them, James Hall and William Brewer.

Chapter Twelve

THE FALL OF RICHMOND AND END OF THE WAR

On April 3rd the glorious news of the fall of Richmond reached us, and that Lee's stubborn army was fast falling back, with Sheridan in hot pursuit.

On April 8th 13 men of Company D, returning from a scout, were fired upon from ambush, Francis T. Bradberry being killed and Isaac H. Metcalf mortally wounded. Our boys returned the fire and killed three of the enemy and wounded others.

Captains Richley and Westlake returned from confederate prisons.

The report reached us today of the surrender of Lee's Army of Northern Virginia, on terms dictated by General Grant. The War Department ordered 200 guns fired at every post in the Union, and our six-pounder at Larkinsville poured out its sweet sound in commemoration of that event.

April 15th our rejoicing was turned into mourning on receipt of the news of the assassination of President Lincoln last night at Ford's Theatre, by J. Wilkes Booth. Our flag was immediately lowered to half mast.

On April 18th guns were fired every half hour from sunrise to sunset, and on the 19th, the day of President Lincoln's funeral, all work in the army was suspended by order of the War Department.

April 24th Colonel Wade and Lieutenant Uptigrove inspected the line of defense from Huntsville to Stevenson. At Brownsboro two companies of the One hundred and eighty-ninth Ohio, under command of Captain Dennis, with detachments from the One hundred and second Ohio and Eighteenth Michigan, were building blockhouses.

The guerrillas kept annoying the patrols and various stations until, on April 26th, Colonel Wade issued an order requiring our men to lay in ambush every other night for the bushwhackers, and on April 29th Frank Cotton's company of guerrillas attempted to capture the patrols of Company D between Woodville and Paint Rock Bridge, when a company of our boys, being in ambush, fired a volley, killing one and wounding three of the enemy.

Company H also lay in ambush for bushwhackers on the 26th, wounding one man and capturing his gun and cap.

By order of General Granger a number of citizens, with Moses A. Morgan as Captain, was authorized to form a military company for defense against the guerrillas. The struggling bands of guerrillas soon began to break up and several came in and surrendered themselves.

Colonel Norwood, formerly of the Fifty-fifth Alabama, communicated with Colonel Wade, asking for leave to come in and surrender on the same terms that were granted General Lee, and after communication with General Granger, Colonel Wade was authorized to accept his surrender on the same terms.

May 7th General Thomas issued an order to the effect that the guerrillas could surrender on the same terms granted to General Lee, and that if they failed to accept and surrender they were henceforth to be treated as outlaws.

News was received about this time of the surrender of General Johnson's forces to General Sherman, and shortly afterwards news was received of the capture of Jeff Davis at Greenville, Ga.

Lieutenant Booher, of Company I, returned to the regiment on May 14th from his imprisonment, and on May 16th the other officers all returned, two years and thirteen days after their separation by capture in Georgia.

On May 25, Companies A, G and K were ordered to Larkinsville, it being considered unnecessary to longer garrison the places where they were stationed, save at Steven's Gap, where 12 men of Company D relieved Company A.

Captain William M. Kendall received his commission as Major, dated May 16th, and he assumed command of the post at Larkinsville, relieving Captain Eaton.

On June 18th Lieutenant-Colonel Wade received his commission as Colonel, and Major Kendall as Lieutenant-Colonel, and on June 10th orders were received for the Seventy-third to go to Nashville for the purpose of being mustered out, and on June 22nd all the companies were concentrated at Larkinsville, the first time the whole regiment had been together for many months.

The wagon train belonging to the regiment was sent overland to Huntsville in charge of Quartermaster Hubbard, to be turned over to the government at that post.

The companies retained their arms and camp equipage until their final muster out.

On June 24th tents were struck preparatory to starting home. Our train arrived late in the afternoon and we reached Huntsville before dark, laying over there until morning by reason of the crowded condition of the road, remaining on the cars all night.

Early on the morning of the 25th we left Huntsville, and reached Nashville about 5 p.m., quartering at the barracks, where we signed muster-out rolls and were mustered out on July 1st by Captain John T. Morris, A.C.M., First Division, Fourth A.C.

The recruits were transferred to the 29th Indiana Regiment. Lieutenant-Colonel Kendall and Lieutenant Williams went on in advance to Louisville to procure transportation to Indianapolis.

On July 2nd we were escorted through the streets of Nashville and left on an extra passenger train at 6:45 p.m., arriving at Louisville at five the next morning.

We marched directly through Louisville, crossed the Ohio River by a ferryboat to Jeffersonville, and took train for Indianapolis, reaching there at six in the afternoon, and were quartered at the Soldiers' Home for the night.

On the 4th we went to "Camp Carrington," and remained there until paid off on July 8th, when the men left on the trains for their respective homes.

On July 4th Colonel Wade issued his last order, as follows:

"Headquarters Seventy-third Indiana Vols,
Indianapolis, Indiana, July 4, 1865.
General Orders, No. 11.

Soldiers: Three years ago you responded to the call of patriotism and marched with full ranks to the field, to battle for the right, to crush the base traitors who had dared to raise a hand against our glorious flag.

Today with sadly thinned ranks, reduced to less than half your original number, your mission fulfilled, you are about to lay down your arms and return to the peaceful pursuits from which you were called away.

Your Commanding Officer cannot let this opportunity pass without expressing to you his heartfelt regret at parting. He desires to assure you that he will ever in after life cherish the recollections that cluster around the march, bivouac, and the battlefield in those eventful three years as the dearest of his life, and to have commanded the Seventy-third Indiana will be his proudest boast.

It were needless for him to dwell upon the scenes in which you have borne a memorable and honorable part. The names upon your banner:

Chaplin Hills,
Stone River,
Day's Cap,
Crooked Creek,
Blount's Farm,
Athens,
Decatur,

and the many skirmishes where death, though not as sweeping, was still sure. "Mill Creek," Franklin Pike," "Limestone Point," "Paint Rock," "Deep Cut," and others, speak in louder, more eloquent terms of your record than words can express, and the long list of brave and gallant spirits from your ranks who have sealed their devotion to their country with their blood, and now sleep in a soldier's grave, are silent witnesses of the part borne by the "Seventy-third" in this struggle for the integrity of our government.

Comrades, as we part now, let each one bear with him to his home the determination to evince in his future life the same manliness, the same fixed purpose to perform your whole duty, the same cheerfulness of disposition which you have so often manifested under trying circumstances in the field, and whatever your occupation may be, success will surely attend you.

To the officers, who, by their hearty cooperation have lightened his load of responsibility, he returns sincere thanks:

With kindest feelings and best wishes for the prosperity and happiness of all, soldiers and comrades, farewell.

By command of
A. B. WADE,
Colonel Seventy-third Indiana, Commanding.
JOSEPH HAGENBUCK, Adjutant."

On July 5th the regiment, in company with others, went to the State House, where Governor Morton made an excellent address, reading a short sketch of the Seventy-third, and where Chaplain Lozier sang "The Good Old Union Wagon" and "Glory Hallelujah," and Major-General Hovey also made an address, followed by Colonel Wade, who expressed his thanks for the honors and favors shown him and his command.

The officers remained at Indianapolis until the 9th,

when they received their pay and disbanded, and the Seventy-third Regiment Indiana Volunteer Infantry, as an organization, came to an end.

Chapter Thirteen

ROSTER

73RD INDIANA VOLUNTEER INFANTRY REGIMENT

REGIMENTAL FIELD & STAFF OFFICERS

Colonels

Gilbert Hathaway: Laporte; Commissioned Aug 21, 1862 ; mustered in Aug 22, 1862; killed in action at Blount's Farm near Gadsden, Ala, May 2, 1863.
Alfred B. Wade: South Bend; Comm. July 6, 1864; mustered out as Lt. Col. Commanding 73rd.

Lieutenant-Colonels

Oliver H. P. Bailey: Plymouth; Comm. Aug 22, 1862; muster Aug 22, 1862; resigned Dec 22, 1862.
Robert W. Graham: Valparaiso; Comm. Feb 13, 1863; muster Feb 14, 1863; resigned Mar 28, 1863; disability.
IVAN N. WALKER: Michigan City; Comm. March 30, 1863; muster July I, 1863; resigned July 4, 1864, disability.
Alfred B. Wade: South Bend; promoted Lt Col July 5, 1864 Commanding 73rd Regt; promoted Colonel, Commanding 73rd Sept 15, 1864;.
William M. Kendall, Plymouth; Comm. July 6, 1864; mustered out as Major with regiment.

Majors

William Krimball: Crown Point; Comm. Aug 21, 1862; muster Aug 22, 1862; resigned Jan 17, 1863 as Capt. Krimball was originator of 73$^{rd.}$
Ivan N. Walker, Michigan City; Comm. Feb 13, 1863; muster Feb 14, 1863; promoted Lt Col.

Alfred B. Wade: South Bend; Comm. Apr 25, 1863; muster July I,1863; promoted Lt. Col.
William M. Kendall: Plymouth; Comm. Sept I, 1864; muster, May 16, 1865; promoted Lt Col..

Adjutants

Oliver H. P. Bailey: Plymouth; Comm. July 18, 1862; Muster Jul 23, 1862; promoted Lt Col.
Alfred B. Wade: South Bend; Comm. Aug 27, 1862 muster Aug 27, 1862; promoted Major.
James C. Woodrow: Plymouth; Comm. Apr 25, 1863; muster Feb 17, 1863; promoted Capt. Co. B; mustered out May 15, 1865; services no longer required.
Joseph Hagenbuck: Laporte; Comm. May I, 1864; muster Nov I, 1864; mustered out with regiment.

Quartermasters

Edward Bacon: South Bend; Comm. Jul. 18, 1862; muster Jul. 21,1862; honorable discharge Sept. 23, 1863.
George M. Hubbard: Logansport; Comm. Oct 24, 1863; muster Nov 1, 1863; mustered out with regiment.

Chaplains

George Guyon: Comm. Dec 31, 1862; muster Jan 8, 1863; resigned Feb 2, 1863.
John A. Frazier: Laporte; Comm. Feb 26, 1863; Muster Feb 26, 1863; resigned Apr 1, 1865.

Surgeons

Robert Spencer: Monticello; Comm. Aug. 21, 1862; muster Aug. 21, 1862; resigned Jan. 21, 1863.
Samuel S. Terry: Rochester; Comm. Jan. 29, 1863; declined.
Tompkins Higday: Laporte; Comm. Feb. 10, 1863; declined.

Seth F. Myers: South Bend; Comm. Mar 18, 1863; muster Mar 24,1863; resigned May 25, 1865; disability.

Assistant Surgeons

Robert Spencer: Monticello; Comm. Jul 16, 1862: muster Jul 27, 1862; promoted Surgeon.
Samuel S. Terry: Rochester; Comm. Sept 27, 1862; resigned October 30, 1862; never mustered.
William H. Brenton: Peru; Comm. Sept 27, 1862; Muster Oct 3, 1862; resigned Mar 13, 1863.
Hiram S. Green: Calumet; Comm. Dec 6, 1862; resigned Jan 14, 1863 as Captain Company E.
Wilson Pottinger: Westville; Comm. Mar 19, 1863; muster Mar 24, 1863; resigned Dec 24, 1863.
William Spencer: Monticello; Comm. Mar 20, 1863; muster Mar 30, 1863; mustered out Apr 18, 1864 for promotion to 10th Tennessee Infantry.
Charles H. Applegate: South Bend; Comm. Jun 30, 1864; muster Nov 13, 1864; mustered out with regiment.

NON-COMMISSIONED STAFF

Sergeant-Majors

John W. Munday
Rufus M. Brown
Gillis J. McBane

Quartermaster-Sergeants

Charles Zutavern
George M. Hubbard
Leander P. Williams
John Holt

Commissary Sergeant

Charles F. Kimball.

Hospital Stewards

James Spencer
Charles H. Applegate
Lourine S. Boyce

Chapter Fourteen

ROSTER, COMPANY A - E

73rd Indiana Volunteer Infantry Regiment

COMPANY A

OFFICERS

Captains

William Krimball: Crown Point; Commission. Aug 5, 1862; mustered August 16, 1862; promoted Major.
Richard W. Price: Lowell; Comm. Aug 22, 1862; resigned Jan 19, 1863.
Alfred Fry: Crown Point; Comm. Aug 30, 1863; promoted May 17, 1865; mustered out with regiment.

1st Lieutenants

Richard W. Price: Lowell; Comm. Aug 5, 1862; muster Aug 16, 1862; promoted Captain.
Philip Reed: Lowell; Comm. August 22, 1862 ; resigned Dec 2, 1862.
Alfred Fry: Crown Point; Comm. Dec 3, 1862; Feb 16, 1863; promoted Captain.
J. Ralph Upthegrove: Crown Point; Comm. Aug 30, 1863; muster May 17, 1865; mustered out with regiment.

Second Lieutenants

Philip Reed: Lowell: Comm. Aug 5, 1862; muster Aug 16, 1862; promoted 1st Lieutenant.
Alfred Fry: Crown Point; Comm. Aug 22, 1862; muster Sept 1, 1862; promoted 1st Lieutenant.
J. Ralph Upthegrove: Crown Point; Comm. Dec 3, 1862; muster Feb 16, 1863; promoted 1st Lieutenant.

George S. Clark: Lowell; Comm. Aug 30, 1863; muster Nov 16, 1863; mustered out and honorably discharged May 17, 1865, as supernumerary.
Oliver G. Wheeler: Crown Point; Comm. Jun 20, 1865; mustered out as 1st Sergeant with regiment.

ENLISTED MEN, COMPANY A

First Sergeants

Fry, Alfred: Crown Point; promoted 2nd Lieutenant.
Wheeler, Oliver G.: Crown Point; mustered out July 1, 1865.

Sergeants

Pratt, Henry: Crown Point; discharged Feb 29, 1863.
Clark, George S.: Lowell; promoted 2nd Lieutenant.
Sprague, Andrew: Crown Point; discharged Nov 25, 1863.
Loving, Thomas W.: Crown Point; died at Nashville, Sept 30, 1863.
Stilson, Asher, Cedar Creek; mustered out Jul 1, 1865.
Farmer, Tunis J., Crown Point; mustered out Jul 1, 1865.
Fowler, Rollin D.: Crown Point; mustered out July 1, 1865.
Farrington, Henry H., Lowell; mustered out Jul 1, 1865.

Corporals

Bray, Joseph: Cedar Creek; discharged Feb 25, 1863.
Graves, Elliot N.: West Creek; discharged Oct 14, 1862.
MORRIS, LEANDER, Calumet; died at Nashville, Tenn., April 30, 1863.
Wheeler, Oliver G.: Crown Point; promoted to 1st Sergeant.
Fuller, Robert W.: Lowell; died at Indianapolis, Aug 2, 1863.
FOWLER, ROLLIN D.: Crown Point; promoted to Sergeant.
Davis, William F.: Cedar Lake; deserted Nov 20, 1862.
BARNEY, DANIEL H.: Cedar Creek; discharged February

25, 1863.
Evans, Evan L., Crown Point; mustered out Jul 1, 1865.
Lidder, Phillip, Chicago, Ill; mustered out Jul 1,1865.
Nichols, Martin, Lowell; mustered out Jul 1,1865.

Musicians

Gordon, Samuel: Deep River; discharged Feb 25, 1863.
Stilson, Charles A.: Cedar Creek; discharge Jan 29, 1863.

Wagoner.

Taylor, William A., Cedar Lake; mustered out Jul 1, 1865.

Privates

Atkins, Lewis, Lowell; died at Nashville, TN, Nov 22, 1862.
Atwood, Eli, Lowell; died at Nashville, TN, Nov 29, 1862.
Ault, Isaac: Lowell; mustered out Jul 1, 1865.
Baughman, Wilson Shannon, Lowell; mustered out Jul 1, 1865. Brother of Pvt./Cpl. Thomas J. Baughman, Co. I.
Bowen, Charles B., Merrillville; discharged Jul 11, 1863.
Boarder, Charles, Winfield; discharged Oct 13, 1862.
Brown, George, Crown Point; discharged Oct, 1863.
Bryant, Arthur V., Lowell; discharged Oct 8, 1863.
Chapman, Oliver A., Crown Point; transferred to VRC Sept 1, 1863.
Childers, John, West Creek; died at Nashville, TN, Dec 3, 1862.
Clark, Alden V., Lowell; discharged Dec 14, 1862.
Colvin, Samuel, Hebron; mustered out Jul 1, 1865.
Curtiss; Theron D., Crown Point; discharged Feb 10, 1863.
Davis, Harvey A., Cedar Creek; deserted Nov 28, 1862.
DeWitt, Orin, Lowell; mustered out Jul 1, 1865, as

Corporal.
Eadus, Newman G., Crown Point; missing in action, Lexington, Ky., Sept 30, 1862.
Early, John H., Crown Point; killed in action at Stones River, Dec 31, 1862.
Evans, Evan L., Crown Point; promoted to Corporal.
Farmer, Tunis J., Crown Point; promoted to Sergeant.
Farrington, Henry H., Lowell; promoted to Sergeant.
Fisher, Phillip, Winfield; discharged Mar 13, 1863.
Fowler, Luman A., Jr., Crown Point; discharged Feb 20, 1863.
Frazier, Alfred K., Merrillville; mustered out Jul 1, 1865.
Frazier, William, Merrillville; died at Nashville, Dec 15, 1862.
Fuller, Jasper M., Lowell; died at Gallatin, TN, Jan 29, 1863.
Fuller, Elisha W., Lowell; discharged Oct 14, 1862.
Gerlach, Michael, Crown Point; transferred to VRC Sept 1, 1863.
Gilbert, Henry, Valparaiso; mustered out Jul 1, 1865.
Gordon, Noah, Wood's Mills; discharged Oct 19, 1862.
Gordonier, Horace, West Creek; mustered out Jul 1, 1865.
Graves, Mariom, West Creek; died at Nashville, Dec 16, 1862.
Granger, William J., Hebron; mustered out Jul 1, 1865.
Green, Lewis, Crown Point; mustered out Jul 1, 1865.
Gregg, Allen, Lowell; mustered out Jul 1, 1865.
Hale, James E., Crown Point; mustered out Jul 1, 1865.
Harkless, Elias, Crown Point; mustered out Jul 1, 1865.
Hathaway, William, West Creek; deserted May 12, 1863.
Holt, John, Crown Point; promoted Quartermaster-Sergeant.
Johann, Peter, Hannah Station; mustered out Jul 1, 1865.
Johnson, Charles, Lowell; discharged Feb 19, 1864.

Jones, Samuel, Lowell; transferred to VRC Oct 24, 1863.
Knoff, Nicholas, Crown Point; discharged Dec 19, 1862.
Kyle, Ransom, Lowell; discharged Apr 18, 1863.
Lamphier, Austin, Crown Point; died at Nashville, Jan 7, 1863.
Lamphier, Lloyd, Crown Point; mustered out Jul 1, 1865.
Lidder, Phillip, Chicago, Ill; promoted to Corporal.
Lill, Jacob, Crown Point; mustered out Jul 1, 1865.
Masseth, Henry, Cedar Creek; mustered out Jul 1, 1865.
Maxwell, John, Merrillville; died at Scottsville, Ky., Nov 9, 1862.
McConn, James, Eagle Creek; mustered out July 1, 1865.
McNay, Alexander, West Creek; discharged Dec 9, 1862.
Metz, George, Cedar Lake; mustered out Jul 1, 1865.
Moore, Isaac W., Crown Point; died at Gallatin, TN, Dec 29, 1862.
Meyers, John F., Crown Point; deserted Dec 1, 1862.
Nichols, Albert, Lowell; died at Nashville, Dec 1, 1862.
Nichols, Martin, Lowell; promoted to Corporal.
Petee, Mortimer, West Creek; mustered out Jul 1, 1865.
Paul, John, Chicago, Ill.; discharged Mar 8, 1863.
Pelton, Milo S., Crown Point; discharged Feb 25, 1863.
Pulver, David, West Creek; discharged Mar 8, 1863.
Roney, James, Merrillville; died, Nashville, Feb 8, 1863.
Rosenbower, John, Crown Point; mustered out Jul 1, 1865.
Sherman, Abel, Crown Point; mustered out Jul 1, 1865.
Smith, John M., Crown Point; discharged Feb 20, 1863.
Sprague, Joseph M., Merrillville; discharged Feb 26, 1862.
Stilson, Asher, Cedar Creek; promoted to Sergeant.
Stowell, John, Lowell; mustered out Jul 1, 1865.
Surprise, Oliver, Lowell; transferred to VRC Oct 24, 1863.
Taylor, DeWitt, Cedar Creek; mustered out Jul 1, 1865.

Tanner, John, Lowell; discharged May 15, 1865.
Toman, George, Crown Point; discharged Mar 20, 1863.
Tremper, William, Crown Point; discharged Dec 15, 1863.
Upthegrove, James H., Crown Point; mustered out Jul 1, 1865.
Upthegrove, J. Ralph, Crown Point; promoted 1st Lt.
Van Burg, Cornelius, Crown Point; died at Bowling Green, Ky., Dec 23, 1862.
Vincent, Mial, Wood's Mill; died at Gallatin, TN, Jan 8, 1863.
Weinant, Philip, St. Johns; mustered out Jul 1, 1865.
Welch, Edward, Winfield; killed in action, Stones River, Dec 31, 1862.
White, Samuel, Crown Point; killed in action, Blount's Farm, Ala., May 2, 1863.
Wise, Benjamin, Winfield; transferred to VRC Sept 1, 1863.
Willis, Benjamin, Lowell; transferred to VRC Aug 29, 1863.
Woods, Edmund, Merrillville; died at Nashville, Nov 29, 1862.

Recruits

Binyon, John, Cedar Lake; transfer to 29th Regt Jul 1, 1865.
Green, Azariah, Hebron; transfer to 29th Regt Jul 1, 1865.
Given, Alexander, Lowell; transfer to 29th Regt Jul 1, 1865.
Laman, George, Crown Point; transfer to 29th Regt Jul 1, 1865.
Mahanny, Amos, Hebron; transfer to 29th Regt Jul 1, 1865.
Metz, Jacob, Cedar Lake; transfer to 29th Regt Jul 1, 1865.
Stilson, Andrew, Cedar Lake; transfer to 29th Regt Jul 1, 1865.

COMPANY B

OFFICERS

Captains

George C. Gladwyn, Laporte; Commission Aug 5, 1862; mustered Aug 16, 1862; resigned Feb 5, 1863.
Theodoric F. C. Dodd, Laporte; Comm. Feb 6, 1863; mustered Feb 6, 1863; resigned Nov 14, 1863.
James C. Woodrow, Plymouth; Comm. May 1, 1864; mustered out and honorably discharged as 1st Lieutenant (Adjutant) May 15, 1865; services no longer required.

First Lieutenants

Theodoric F. C. Dodd, Laporte; Comm. Aug 5, 1862; muster Aug 16, 1862; promoted Captain.
Joseph Hagenbuck, Laporte; Comm. Feb 6, 1863; muster Nov I, 1863 ; promoted Adjutant.
John W. Munday, Laporte; Comm. May I, 1864; resigned as 2d Lieutenant May 26, 1865; cause, business affairs.
James H. Kiersted, Laporte; Comm. May 27, 1865; muster June 29, 1865; mustered out with regiment.

Second Lieutenants

Joseph Hagenbuck, Laporte; Comm. Aug 5, 1862; Muster Aug 16, 1862; promoted 1st Lieutenant.
John W. Munday, Laporte; Comm. Feb 6, 1863; muster March 6, 1863; promoted 1st Lieutenant.
James H. Kiersted, Laporte; May I, 1864; May 20, 1864; promoted 1st Lieutenant.

ENLISTED MEN, COMPANY B

First Sergeants

Munday, John W., Laporte; promoted 2nd Lieutenant.
Walker, Obediah, Hudson; mustered out Jul 1,1865.

Commissary Sergeant

Kimball, Charles F., Laporte; muster out July 1, 1865.

Sergeants

Penwell, Lewis T., Laporte; mustered out July I, 1865.
Drown, Thomas E., Hudson; died Nashville, TN., Feb 1863.
Boyce, Lourine S., Laporte; discharged Nov 29, 1862; disability.
Kiersted, James H., Laporte; promoted 2d Lt.
Powell, Walter, Laporte; mustered out Jul 1, 1865.
Western, Charles B., Laporte; muster out Jul 1, 1865.

Corporals

Hoover, George, Laporte; mustered out Jul 1, 1865 as Private.
Powell, Walter, Laporte; promoted to Sergeant.
Hicks, Jonas L., Hudson; discharged Oct 3, 1863.
Paddock, Thomas I., No. Buffalo, Mich; discharged Apr 8, 1863.
Frazier, Thomas, Laporte; died, Cincinnati, Ohio, Jan 1863.
Bentz, Frank, Laporte; mustered out Jul 1, 1865.
Graham, Charles E., Laporte; deserted at Columbia, Ky., Oct 25,1862.
Walker, Obediah, Hudson; promoted to 1st Sergeant.
Bowin, Alexander, Laporte; mustered out Jul 1, 1865.
Colman, John, Laporte; mustered out Jul 1, 1865.
Marble, Miner S., Laporte; mustered out Jul 1, 1865.

Musicians

Wells, Americus, Springville; discharged Jun 9, 1863.
Wells, Hannibal, Springville; died at Louisville, Ky., Aug 26, 1862.

Wagoner

Mix, Elon, Laporte; died at New Albany, Ind., 1862.
Lenhart, Jacob, Hudson; mustered out Jul 1, 1865.

Privates

Ballaw, Ambrose, Hudson; died at Nashville, TN, Dec 20, 1863.
Beuford, William, Laporte; died at Nashville, TN, Feb 9, 1863.
Bentley, Orris, No. Buffalo, Mich; mustered out Jul 1, 1865.
Berkstahler, August, Laporte; discharged Mar 27, 1863.
Bishop, Elihu, No. Buffalo, Mich; mustered out Jul 1, 1865.
Bogardus, William B., Laporte; transferred to V.R.C. Oct 30, 1863.
Bowin, Alexander, Laporte; promoted to Corporal.
Bowin, Benton, Laporte; discharged Mar 27, 1863.
Briggs, Francis W., Laporte; discharged Jan 2, 1863.
Bulhand, Charles L., New Carlisle; mustered out Jul 1, 1865.
Burlet, Joseph A., Laporte; discharged Apr 22, 1863.
Cassada, William L., Hudson; discharged Nov 4, 1862.
Claybaugh, Thomas, Plymouth; transferred to V.R.C. Oct 20, 1863.
Clark, Horace, Hudson; mustered out Jul 1, 1865.
Colman, John, Laporte; promoted to Corporal.
Collor, Henry, Laporte; died, Nashville, TN, Dec 11, 1862.
Collor, Luther, Laporte; died,Nashville, TN, Dec 11, 1862.

Cooper, William, Laporte; discharged Oct 26, 1863.
Coppock, Nathan W., Laporte; discharged Nov 1862.
Cornelius, Ephraim C., Hudson; died, Nashville, TN, Aug 12, 1863.
Cross, James, Springville; discharged Jul 4, 1864.
Davidson, Giles, Springville; died, Gallatin, TN., Dec 14, 1862.
Drown, John W., Hudson; deserted at Louisville, Ky., Feb 10, 1863.
Dolph, David, Springville; died, Murfreesboro, TN, Apr 15, 1863.
Easten, William P., Springville; died, Nashville, TN, Apr 14, 1863.
Fields, Lorenzo, Springville; mustered out Jul 1, 1865.
Frazier, Milton E., Laporte; discharged Feb 28, 1863.
Freeze, Christopher, Laporte; mustered out Jul 1, 1865.
Harrington, Henry, No. Buffalo, Mich; mustered out Jul 1, 1865.
Harris, Levitus, Laporte ; mustered out Jul 1, 1865.
Hays, Thomas, Detroit, Mich.; mustered out Jul 11, 1865.
Haynes, Francis D., Springville; mustered out Jul 1, 1865.
Holden, Henry, No. Buffalo, Mich.
Huntley, Henry E., Springville; discharged Dec 26, 1863.
Jeffreys, John, Laporte; deserted at Laporte, Ind., Jun 16, 1863.
Jennison, Charles, Laporte; transferred to V.R.C. Jun 30, 1863.
Josling, Henry, Laporte.
Kaffling, John, No. Buffalo, Mich; died at Lookout Mountain, TN, Dec 19, 1864.
Kimball, Charles F., Laporte; promoted to Commissary Sergeant.
Lamb, Orrin C., Laporte; deserted at Gallatin, TN, Nov 9, 1862.
Lamb, Jonathan E., Laporte; deserted at Gallatin, TN., Nov 9, 1862.
Lay, Sebastian, Laporte; mustered out Jul 1, 1865.
Lee, William S., Laporte; discharged November 19, 1862.
Leanland, Victoria W., Laporte; muster out Jul 1, 1865.
Lenhart, Jacob, Hudson; promoted to Wagoner.

Lenhart, Elias, Hudson; died, Gallatin, TN, Dec 24, 1862.
Lucher, Samuel, Laporte; deserted at Lexington, Ky., Sept 1, 1862.
Mandeville, Daniel B., Laporte; discharged Jan 13, 1863.
Marble, Miner S., Laporte; promoted to Corporal.
Moore, Samuel, Springville; mustered out Jul 1, 1865,
Mott, Alva, Laporte; deserted Oct 25, 1862; returned March 3, 1864.
McMellen, Mathew, Roselle; mustered out Jul 1, 1865.
O'Brian, James
Olin, Clifford, Laporte; transferred to V.R.C. Dec 3, 1863.
Oliver, Albert, Springville; mustered out Jul 1, 1865.
Phillipps, Christian, Hudson; discharged Jan 21, 1864.
Perry, Edward I., Laporte; discharged Nov 29, 1862.
Rodgers, Willard D. S., Hudson; discharged Feb 15, 1864.
Seymore, Mortimer, Laporte.
Shade, Willam, Laporte; died at Gallatin, TN, Feb 24, 1863.
Sherman, George, Laporte; died at Gallatin,TN, Feb 1863.
Sherwood, Albert, Laporte; mustered out Jul 1, 1865.
Shults, Henry, Springville; mustered out July 1, 1865.
Shippy, George W., No. Buffalo, Mich; deserted.
Stanton, Judah L., Laporte; discharged Mar 3, 1863.
Styles, Hezekiah, Springville; died at Triana, Ala., Oct 17, 1864.
Stotts, Mayze, Laporte; died at Nashville, TN, Feb 16, 1863.
Smith, Alvin H., Laporte; discharged Jul 22, 1863.
Tuttle, Jerome, No. Buffalo, Mich; died at Nashville, TN, Nov 5, 1862.
Vader, Allen, No. Buffalo, Mich; mustered out Jul 1, 1865.
Vader, Daniel, No. Buffalo, Mich; muster out Jul 1, 1865.
Warner, Croyden, Springville; mustered out Jul 1, 1865.

Waxham, Walter. A., Laporte; died at Nashville, TN, Dec 7, 1862.
Western, Charles B., Laporte; promoted to Sergeant.
Westfall, George, South Bend; died near Nashville, TN, Dec 5, 1862.
Whitbrook, Frederick, Laporte; muster out Jul 1, 1865.
White, Benjamin S., Springville; muster out Jul 1, 1865.
Williams, Isaiah, Hudson; mustered out Jul 1, 1865.
Winchell, Ralph, Laporte; died at Nashville, TN, Dec 8, 1863.
Wright, Stanton, No. Buffalo, Mich.; deserted at Gallatin, TN, Nov 9, 1862.
Zimmerman, Jacob, Laporte; muster out Jul 1, 1865.
Zell, Frederick J., Laporte; discharged.

Recruits

Boyce, Laurin S., Laporte; transfer to 29th Regt Jul 1, 1865.
Dixon, Jacob, transfer to 29th Regt Jul 1, 1865.
Hawley, Price W., Laporte; transfer to 29th Regt Jul 1, 1865.
Paxon, John W., South Bend; discharged Mar 1, 1863.
York, Robert J., Laporte; transfer to 29th Regt Jul 1, 1865.
Young, Philip L., Laporte, transfer to 29th Regt Jul 1, 1865.

COMPANY C

OFFICERS

Captains

Charles W. Price, South Bend; Commission Aug 5, 1862; muster Aug 16, 1862; resigned Nov 24, 1862.
John A. Richley, South Bend; Comm. Nov 25, 1862; muster Feb 16, 1863; mustered out with regiment.

First Lieutenants

John A. Richley, South Bend; Comm. Aug 5, 1862; muster Aug 16, 1862; promoted Captain.
Alexander N. Thomas, South Bend; Comm. Nov 25, 1862; muster Feb 17, 1863; mustered out with regiment.

Second Lieutenants

John G. Greenawalt, Plymouth; Comm. Aug 5, 1862; muster Aug 16, 1862; discharged May 9, 1864, on account of wounds received in action.
John Y. Slick, South Bend; Comm. May 25, 1864; muster Sept 1, 1864; mustered out with regiment.

ENLISTED MEN, COMPANY C

First Sergeants

Finley, James B., South Bend; died near Murfreesboro, Jan 28, 1863.
Cole, Benjamin R., North Liberty; mustered out Jul 1, 1865.

Sergeants

Pearson, Lorenzo, South Bend; mustered out Jul 1, 1865 as private.
Clemens, Charles W., South Bend; killed in Military Prison, Jul 1863.
Pierce, John M., South Bend; transferred to Marine Service Mar 1, 1863.
Ruple, John W., North Liberty; discharged Feb 26, 1863; disability.
Annis, Augustus, South Bend; mustered out Jul 1, 1865.
Morgan, Henry C., South Bend; mustered out Jul 1, 1865.
Streets, James B., South Bend; died at Scottsville, Ky., Nov 6,1 1865.
Romig, John A., South Bend; mustered out Jul 1, 1865.

Corporals

Romig, John A., South Bend; promoted to Sergeant.
Teel, John W., South Bend; mustered out Jul 1, 1865.
Cole, Benjamin R., North Liberty; promoted to 1st Sergeant.
Faurote, Nathaniel F., Terre Coupee; mustered out Jul 1, 1865.
Brown, George S., Walkerton; discharged Sept 29, 1863; disability.
Trueblood, William, South Bend; died at Nashville, TN, Dec 16 1862.
Thomas, Alexander N., South Bend; promoted to First Lieutenant.
Kendall, Howard L., Niles, Mich; mustered out May 3, 1865.
Finch, Newton M., South Bend; muster out Jul 1, 1865.
Frame, Allen, South Bend; mustered out Jul 1, 1865.

Houser, David M., Lakeville; muster out Jul 1, 1865.

Musicians

Gorsuch, Wilber E., South Bend; mustered out Jul 1, 1865.
Hall, James F., South Bend; mustered out Jul 1, 1865.

Wagoner

Cotton, Gregory H., South Bend; killed by accidental shot, Oct 2, 1864.

Privates

Annis, Augustus, South Bend; promoted to Sergeant.
Babcock, Hiram, South Bend; killed in action Dec 31, 1862, Stones River.
Ballou, Albert, South Bend; discharged Mar 20, 1863; disability.
Ballou, Orin, Mishawaka; mustered out Jul 1, 1865.
Barr, Samuel T., South Bend; discharged Oct 19, 1863; disability.
Bivins, Joseph, Plymouth; discharged Sept 24, 1864; disability.
Brewer, William H., South Bend; discharged Jun 18, 1865; wounds.
Brewer, John, South Bend; died near Murfreesboro, TN, Feb 15, 1863.
Brittenhham, John, Lakeville; killed in action at Stones River, Dec 31, 1862.
Brown, Mahlon, Byron, O.; died at Bowling Green, Ky., Jan 5, 1863.
Burden, Nathaniel, Terre Coupee; mustered out Jul 1865.
Brumfield, Stanton J., Lakeville; transferred to VRC. Oct 1, 1863.
Burk, Milton M., Walkerton; discharged Dec 10, 1862; disability.
Clark, John, Lakeville; transferred to VRC Oct 1, 1863.

Curtis, James A., Walkerton; mustered out Jul 1, 1865.
Davis, Andrew, South Bend; transfer to VRC Oct I, 1863.
Dively, Lorenzo, North Liberty; died at Danville, Ky., Dec 1, 1862.
Dively, George, North Liberty; died at Nashville, Nov 21, 1862.
Eaton, James R., South Bend; transfer to VRC Nov 9, 1862.
Fetzer, John, North Liberty; mustered out Jul 1, 1865.
Finch, Newton M., South Bend; promoted to Corporal.
Finney, Abram, San Pierre; killed by accidental shot, Feb 6, 1865.
Finney, Egbert, San Pierre; muster out Jul 1, 1865.
Frame, Allen, South Bend; promoted to Corporal.
Frazer, John A., South Bend; muster out Jul 1, 1865.
Fullmer, William M., North Liberty; died Feb 11,1863; wounds received at Stones River.
Gilvey, Michael, San Francisco, CA; deserted Nov 16, 1862.
Herring, Henry, South Bend; muster out Jul 1, 1865.
Henry, John, Lakeville; died at Rick's River, Ky, Oct 16, 1862.
Huey, William H., South Bend; died at Nashville, Feb 3, 1863.
Hinebaugh, Jacob, South Bend; died near Glasgow, Ky., Nov 18, 1862.
Hoover, William B., South Bend; transfer to VRC Nov 1, 1863.
Hosler, Christian, South Bend; deserted Aug 20, 1862.
Houser, David M., Lakeville; promoted to Corporal.
Huber, John, South Bend; discharged Mar 13, 1864; disability.
King, Christian, South Bend; muster out Jul 1, 1865.
Jay, Barton. H., Terre Coupee; muster out Jul 1, 1865.
Lane, Ephraim T., South Bend; killed at Stones River, Dec 31, 1862.
Lario, Lewis, South Bend; mustered out Jul 1, 1865.
Ledwick, James, South Bend; mustered out Jul 1, 1865.
Limbeck, Simon, South Bend; discharged Mar 4, 1865;

disability.
Liggett, Joseph, Walkerton; mustered out Jul 1, 1865.
Lonzo, Moses, South Bend; discharged Jan 10, 1863; wounds, Stones River.
Loy, Jacob, Walkerton; discharged Apr 29, 1863; wounds, Stones River.
Magdeburg, Guido, South Bend; mustered out Jul 1, 1865.
Mapes, John J., South Bend; died at Louisville, Ky., Jul 17, 1863.
Marter, Samuel D., South Bend; discharged Jun 25, 1863; wounds, Stones River.
Marter, Ezra, South Bend; transfer to VRC Oct 1, 1863.
Matthes, George, South Bend; muster out Jul 1, 1865.
May, John, Rochester, OH; transferred 18th U. S. Infantry Dec 1, 1862.
McDaniel, John W., Walkerton; muster out Jul 1, 1865.
McGoggy, Elijah K., Walkerton; deserted Nov 4, 1862.
McGowan, William, Buchanan, Mich; discharged Mar 30, 1863; disability.
McLloyd, Joseph F., Terre Coupee; transfer to Marine Service Mar 1, 1863.
Miller, Jeremiah F., South Bend; mustered out Jul 1865.
Miller, John H., New Carlisle; transfer Marine Service Mar 1, 1863.
Moon, William H., Lakeville; killed in action at Stones River, Dec 31, 1862.
Morgan, Henry C., South Bend; promoted to Sergeant.
O'Connor, John, N. Buffalo, Mich; discharged Aug 20, 1864; disability.
Parrish, William T., Walkerton; died at Louisville, Ky, Dec 10, 1862.
Paul, George, Walkerton; died Jan 2, 1863; wounds, Stones River.
Pearson, Hiram, South Bend; died at Danville, Ky., Nov 9, 1862.
Quigley, John V., Walkerton; died at Harrodsburg, Ky, Nov 9, 1862.
Quigley, George W., North Liberty; deserted Oct 23, 1862.
Roof, William, Lakeville; discharged Feb 6, 1863;

disability.
Rose, Asbury, Walkerton; mustered out Jul 1, 1865.
Schiller, Daniel, South Bend; mustered out Jul 1, 1865.
Schreffler, Tiras, South Bend; discharged Jun 20, 1864.
Shultz, John B., South Bend; discharged Jan 20, 1864; disability.
Slick, John Y., South Bend; promoted 2nd Lt, Co C..
Streets, James B., South Bend; promoted to Sergeant.
Steele, Austin, Laporte; mustered out Jul 1, 1865.
Stone, Frederick, Hamilton; discharged May 23, 1863; wounds, Stones River.
Swank, Conrad, North Liberty; died at Louisville, Ky., Dec 11, 1862.
Teel, Moses, South Bend; died Jan 19, 1863; wounds received Stones River.
Thompson, John M., South Bend; died at Gallatin, TN, Nov 29, 1862.
Turner, Melvin F., South Bend; deserted Aug 25, 1862.
Vangeison, Richard A., South Bend; discharged Oct 1862; disability.
Zu Tavern, Charles, Springfield, OH; discharged Mar 11, 1863; disability.

Recruits

Burden, Nathaniel; transfer 29th Regt Jul 1, 1865.
Cothin, Woodford; transfer 29th Regt Jul 1, 1865.
Hughley, Thomas M.; transfer 29th Regt Jul 1, 1865.
Polk, William S.; transfer 29th Regt Jul 1, 1865.
Roberts, Levi; transfer 29th Regt Jul 1,1865.
Moore, John; transfer 29th Regt Jul 1, 1865.

COMPANY D

OFFICERS

Captains

William M. Kendall, Plymouth; Commission Aug 5, 1862; mustered Aug 16, 1862: promoted Major.
James M. Beeber, Rochester; Comm. Sept 1, 1864; muster May 16, 1865; mustered out with regiment.

First Lieutenants

John H. Beeber, Rochester; Comm. Aug 5, 1862; muster Aug 16, 1862; resigned Apr 15, 1864.
Winfield S. Ramsay, Plymouth; Comm. Sept 1, 1864; muster Nov 7, 1864; mustered out with regiment.

Second Lieutenants

William T. Grimes, Gilead; Comm. Aug 5, 1862; muster Aug 16, 1862; resigned Jul 25, 1864; cause, for the good of the service.
Rufus M. Brown, Plymouth; Sept 1, 1864; mustered out as Sergeant with regiment.

ENLISTED MEN, COMPANY D

First Sergeants

Beeber, James M., Plymouth; promoted Captain Sept 1, 1864.
Cook, William G., Plymouth; promoted from Corporal to 1st Sergeant. mustered out Jul 1, 1865

Sergeants

Shidler, Noah, Plymouth; mustered out Jul 1, 1865.
Haggerty, Perry C., Plymouth; mustered out Jul 1, 1865.

Newhouse, Thomas, Plymouth; mustered out Jul 1, 1865.
Brown, Rufus M., Plymouth; mustered out Jul l, 1865.

Corporals

Case, John H., Plymouth; died at Gallatin, TN, Dec 29, 1862.
Ramsay, Winfield S., Plymouth; promoted 1st Lieutenant.
Reed, William H. H., Bourbon; mustered out Jul 1, 1865.
Primley, Senica, Plymouth; discharged Apr 9, 1863; wounds received at Stones River.
Jackson, Daniel W., Plymouth; mustered out Jul 1, 1865.
Cook, William G., Plymouth; promoted to 1st Sergeant.
Simons, William H . H., Plymouth; mustered out Jul 1, 1865.
Gibson, James M., Plymouth; mustered out Jul 1, 1865.
Barnhill, Ezra K., Argos; promoted from Private to Corporal; mustered out Jul 1, 1865.
Cox, Fernando, Argos; promoted from Private to Corporal; mustered out Jul 1, 1865.
Stanley, Robert C., Plymouth; promoted from Private to Corporal; mustered out Jul 1, 1865.
Whittaker, John, Argos; promoted from Private to Corporal; mustered out July 1, 1865.

Musicians

Heyney, David, Plymouth; deserted Oct 5, 1863.
Umhols, John, Plymouth; mustered out Jul 1, 1865.

Wagoner

Kreighbaum, Cyrus, Plymouth; died at hospital at Louisville, Ky., Jan 19, 1864.

Privates

Allen, Henry H., Plymouth; mustered out Jul 1, 1865.
Albert, Jonas, Plymouth; deserted Sept 1, 1862.
Barnhill, Ezra K., Argos; promoted to Corporal.

Beeber, Samuel O., Rochester; muster out Jul 1, 1865.
Behner, Francis M., Bourbon; died at Lebanon, Ky., Nov 1862.
Bendure, John, Bourbon; died at Gallatin, TN, Jan 16, 1863.
Bent, Benjamin, Plymouth; discharged Mar 26, 1863 ; disability.
Blasingham, Thomas A., Inwood; muster out Jul 1, 1865.
Bright, William R., Inwood; discharged Jan 5, 1863; disability.
Bright, Richard, Inwood; discharged Jan 1, 1863; disability.
Broadstone, John, Plymouth; muster out Jul 1, 1865.
Borton, Job, Argos; mustered out Jul 1, 1865.
Bucher, Christopher, Argos; killed in action Stones River, Dec 31, 1862.
Burns, Benjamin, Argos; mustered out Jul 1, 1865.
Burden, Thomas, Plymouth; mustered out Jul 1, 1865.
Bowel, Andrew J., Argos; mustered out Jul 1, 1865.
Bowen, Stephen J., Plymouth; discharged Feb 20, 1862; disability.
Clem, James E., Plymouth; mustered out Jul 1, 1865.
Cox, Fernando, Argos; mustered out Jul 1, 1865 as Corporal.
Covert, William P. B., Plymouth; mustered out Jul 1, 1865.
Cruzan, Oliver H., Plymouth; died at Nashville, TN, Dec 29, 1862.
Crum, Daniel, Plymouth; died at Murfreesboro, TN, Mar 25, 1863.
Downs, James H., Plymouth; mustered out Jul 1, 1865.
Dunlap, William T., Plymouth; discharged Feb 20, 1863; disability.
Evans, Joseph, Argos; mustered out Jul 1, 1865.
Flora, George, Plymouth; discharged Feb 20, 1863; disability.
Foster, Zepheniah, Plymouth; discharged Jan 1, 1863; disability.
Gilson, Thomas, Plymouth; mustered out Jul 1, 1865.

Gilson, William, Bourbon; transfer to VRC Oct 23, 1863.
Gilson, John, Plymouth; mustered out Jul 1, 1865.
Gerrard, George W., Inwood; mustered out Jul 1, 1865.
Green, Benjamin F., Plymouth; deserted Mar 1, 1865.
Greer, George W., Plymouth; transfer to VRC Jan 1, 1865.
Griggs, Ephraim, Plymouth; mustered out Jul 1, 1865.
Griggs, George W., Plymouth; transferred to VRC Oct 25, 1863.
Hendricks, Thomas J., Plymouth; died at Nashville, TN, Dec 11, 1862.
Hindel, John T., Inwood; mustered out Jun 18, 1865.
Henry, William L. B., Plymouth; died at Nashville, TN, Dec 15, 1862.
Hooker, William, Argos; mustered out Jul 1, 1865.
Holm, Adam, Plymouth; deserted Sept, 1862.
Kaiser, William H., Bourbon; muster out Jul 1, 1865.
Kaufman, George W., Plymouth; muster out July 1, 1865.
Keller, John, Bourbon; mustered out Jul 1, 1865.
Leak, Thomas, Argos; discharged Aug 8, 1863; disability.
Latham,. Henry A., Plymouth; deserted Aug 17, 1862.
McCoy, William H., Argos; mustered out Jul 1, 1865.
McGriff, David, Argos; mustered out Jul 1, 1865.
McGriff, Simon, Argos; mustered out Jul 1, 1865.
McDonald, James, Plymouth; died at Nashville, TN, Dec 15, 1862.
McLaughlin, Harrison, Argos; mustered out Jul 1, 1865.
Maxey, John A., Plymouth; mustered out Jul 1, 1865.
Newhouse, Wilber F., Argos; mustered out Jul 1, 1865.
Oaf, Jonathan, Plymouth; deserted Sept 25, 1862.
Payne, Martin V., Inwood; discharged Jan 1, 1863.
Piper, Anderson D., Bourbon; transferred to U. S. Artillery Jan 4, 1863.
Pfeiffer, Jacob, Plymouth; discharged Jan 1, 1863.
Plotner, Conrad, Inwood; discharged Jan 30, 1863.

Pomeroy, Smith, Plymouth; mustered out Jul 1, 1865.
Reilley, Lewis S., Bourbon; died at Crabb Orchard, Ky., Oct 28, 1862.
Reilley, John, Bourbon; mustered out May 15, 1865.
Reighley, Edward, Inwood; discharged Jan 1, 1863.
Reed, Anson, Bourbon; discharged May 8, 1863.
Rhodes, Michael, Argos; discharged Jan 1, 1863.
Stanley, Robert C., Plymouth; promoted to Corporal.
Stanley, Francis C., Plymouth; mustered out Jul 1, 1865.
Sapp, John H., Plymouth; mustered out Jul 1, 1865.
Stafford, William, Argos; mustered out Jul 1, 1865.
Smith, Philip, Plymouth; mustered out Jul 1, 1865.
Smith, Benjamin F., Plymouth; transferred to VRC Oct 23, 1863. .
Sluyter, Asa P., Plymouth; captured near Tennessee River, Sept 29, 1864.
Taber, Henry C., Plymouth; mustered out Jul 1, 1865.
Tribby, John W., Argos; died in hospital, Silver Springs, Ky., Nov 19, 1862.
Warfield, George W., Plymouth; died in hospital, Murfreesboro, Mar 4, 1863.
Watson, Martin, Plymouth; discharged Dec 14, 1862.
Wilcox, Charles H., Plymouth; mustered out Jul 1, 1865.
Wilson, William E., Plymouth; died near Nashville, Dec 6, 1862.
Walker, Marion, Plymouth; deserted September 1862.
Webb, Francis D., Plymouth; transferred into 73d Regiment, Jul 31, 1864.
White, Joseph, Plymouth; mustered out Jul 1, 1865.
Whittaker, John, Argos; promoted to Corporal.
World, Otto, South Bend; mustered out Jul 1, 1865.
Yost, Lawrence, Plymouth; mustered out Jul 1, 1865.

Recruits

Berry, Johnson, Argos; transfer to VRC Jan 16, 1862.
Black, William H., Salem; transfer to 29th Regt Jul 1, 1865.

Barley, Thomas J., Bradford; transfer to 29th Regt Jul 1, 1865.
Bradberry, Francis T., Fredricksburg; killed in action near Jackson, Ala., Apr 8, 1865.
Burk, Enoch, Indianapolis; deserted May 28, 1864.
Bunch, James, Bradford; deserted Apr 1, 1864.
Beeber, George H., Indianapolis; transfer to 29th Regt Jul 1, 1865.
Cramer, Benjamin W., Plymouth; transfer to 29th Regt Jul 1, 1865.
Connell, Charles C., Lafayette; transfer to 29th Regt Jul 1, 1865.
Dawson, William H. H., Argos; transfer to 29th Regt Jul 1, 1865.
Gordon, John A., Argos; transfer to 29th Regt Jul 1, 1865.
Gordon, Daniel, Argos; transfer to 29th Regt Jul 1, 1865.
Hughs, Taylor, Sparksville; transfer to 29th Regt Jul 1, 1865.
Jones, William C., Palmyra; transfer to 29th Regt Jul 1, 1865.
Lowry, Alfred B., Argos; transfer to 29th Regiment Jul 1, 1865.
Lowry, John A., Argos; transfer to 29th Regt Jul 1, 1865.
Loosman, George, Medora; transfer to 29th Regt Jul 1, 1865.
Mitcalf, Isaac H., Greenville; died Apr 23, 1865; wounds received in action.
Moore, John, Milltown; transfer to 29th Regt Jul 1, 1865.
Owen, Joel, Newport; deserted Mar 26, 1864.
Porter, Henry W.; transfer to 29th Regt Jul 1, 1865.
Poe, Jonathan, Milltown; transfer to 29th Regt Jul 1, 1865.
Rice, John A.; transfer to 29th Regt Jul 1, 1865.
Riseing, Peter, Palmyra; transfer to 29th Regt Jul 1, 1865.
Riseing, Michael, Greenville; transfer to 29th Regt Jul l, 1865.
Starkey, Asa, Argos; transfer to 29th Regt Jul 1, 1865.
Spencer, James J., Argos; transfer to 29th Regt Jul 1,

1865.
Spencer, John, Argos; mustered out Aug 4, 1865.
Scott, John D., Argos ; died in hospital at Athens, Ala., Oct 23, 1864.
Wilson, Peter, Indianapolis; deserted Mar 7, 1864.
Wright, John, Hardinsburg; mustered out Jul 23, 1865.
Walker, Nicholas O., Triana; mustered out May 16, 1865.

COMPANY E

OFFICERS,

Captains

Hiram Green, Calumet; Commission Aug 5, 1862; muster Aug 16, 1862; promoted Assistant Surgeon.
Albert A. Carley, Michigan City; Comm. Feb 13, 1863; muster Feb 17, 1863; wounded and captured at Day's Gap, Ala., Apr 30, 1863; supposed to be dead.

First Lieutenants

Garrett G. Seeger, Calumet; Comm. Aug 5, 1862; muster Aug 16, 1862; resigned Jan 22, 1863.
John L. Brown, Calumet; Comm. Feb 13, 1863; muster Feb 17, 1863; mustered out with regiment.

Second Lieutenants

Henry H. Tillotson, Calumet; Comm. Aug 5, 1862; muster Aug 16, 1862; mustered out and honorably discharged May 15, 1865; services no longer required.
Charles W. Wheeler, Calumet; Comm. Jun 20, 1865; mustered out as 1st Sergeant with regiment.

ENLISTED MEN, COMPANY E

First Sergeants

Carley, Alberta A., Calumet; promoted to Captain.
Wheeler, Charles W., Calumet; mustered out Jul 1, 1864.

Sergeants

Fletter, Benjamin F., Calumet; discharged Dec 5, 1862; disability.

Thomas, John S., Calumet; deserted Nov 1, 1862.
Wheeler, Charles W., Calumet; promoted to 1st Sergeant.
Brown, John L., Calumet; promoted 1st Lieutenant.
Cooley, Peter, Calumet; mustered out Jul 1, 1865.
Cole, John C., Calumet; mustered out Jul 1, 1865.
Fisher, George, Calumet; mustered out July 1, 1865.

Corporals

Whitmore, Andrew, Calumet; deserted in face of enemy, April 30, 1863.
Beck, George W., Calumet; transferred to Invalid Corps.
Storms, Judson D., Calumet; mustered out Jul 1, 1865 as private.
Cooley, Peter, Calumet; promoted to Sergeant.
Lynd, Leonard E., Calumet; transferred to VRC.
Bostwick, Samuel, Calumet; discharged.
Kindig, Jesse, Calumet; died at Nashville, TN, Dec 4, 1862.
Flood, John, Calumet; discharged.
Beck, Jacob C., Calumet; mustered out Jul 1, 1865.
Curtis, Charles C., Calumet; mustered out Jul 1, 1865.
Demoss, Nathan, Calumet; mustered out Jul 1, 1865.
Osborn, Daniel L., Calumet; mustered out Jul 1, 1865.
Ritter, John J., Calumet; mustered out Jul 1, 1865.

MUSICIANS

Pratt, Moses G. J., Calumet; mustered out.
Pratt, Charles A., Calumet; muster out Jul 1, 1865.

Wagoner

Shurburn, Calvin C., Calumet; discharged Feb 28, 1865; disability.

Privates

Anderson, John, Calumet; died at Murfreesboro, TN, Mar 21, 1863.

Beebe, McGeorge, Calumet; mustered out Jul 1, 1865.
Beck, Jacob C., Calumet; promoted to Corporal.
Beck, Andrew, Calumet; died at Gallatin, TN, Feb 9, 1863.
Brewer, Lemuel, Calumet; mustered out Jul 1, 1865.
Brown, Lewis, Calumet; mustered out Jul 1, 1865.
Brown Christopher, Calumet; mustered out Jul 1, 1865.
Brumley, William, Calumet; discharged.
Burrows, Thomas C., Calumet; deserted May 25, 1863.
Burstrum, Frank, Calumet; mustered out Jul 1, 1865.
Castle, Alfred A., Calumet; discharged Dec 16, 1862; disability.
Curtis, Charles C., Calumet; promoted to corporal.
Crane, Edward, Calumet; deserted Sept 22, 1863.
Cooley, George W., Calumet; mustered out Jul 1, 1865.
Coulson, Chauncy R., Calumet; died at Jeffersonville, Ind., Feb 1, 1865.
Conklin, Isaac, Calumet; discharged Mar 5, 1863; disability.
Cole, Andrew J., Calumet; discharged Apr 4, 1863; disability.
Cole, David P., Calumet; discharged Dec 26, 1862; disability.
Cole, John C., Calumet; promoted to Sergeant.
Chrisman, Isaac, Calumet; discharged Jul 15, 1863; disability.
Chrisman, Addison, Calumet; mustered out Jul 1, 1865.
Chrisman, Oliver, Calumet; discharged Jul 15, 1863; disability.
Demoss, Nathan, Calumet; promoted to Corporal.
Errickson, Nelse A., Calumet; died at Scottsville, Ky. Nov 11, 1862.
Estes, John, Calumet; mustered out.
Fisher, George, Calumet; promoted to Sergeant.
Fox, Josiah B., Calumet; died at Bowling Green, Ky. Feb 27, 1863.
Fuller, John B., Calumet; mustered out Jul 1, 1865.
Gibbons, Richard, Calumet; mustered out Jul 1, 1865.
Glazier, Asa, Calumet; died at Louisville, Ky, Dec 8,

1862.
Green, Lean, Calumet; discharged Dec 26, 1862; insanity.
Gustafson, Adolph, Calumet; discharged Feb 27, 1863; disability.
Hitchcock, Lester B., Calumet; died at Danville, Ky, Dec 8, 1862.
Hineline, John, Calumet; died at Scottsville, Ky., Nov 17, 1862.
Holland, James J., Calumet; mustered out Jul 1, 1865.
Hough, Charles B., Calumet; discharged Jul 17, 1863; disability.
Isaacson, Andrew, Calumet; discharged Apr 21, 1863; disability.
Jackson, Robert, Calumet; killed in action at Day's Gap, Ala., Apr 30, 1863.
Johnson, Augustus, Calumet; discharged Dec 1 1862; disability.
Johnson, Andrew, Calumet; died at Indianapolis, Oct 23, 1863.
Johnson, Clans, Calumet; deserted Jun 17, 1863.
Ketchum, Charles E., Calumet; mustered out Jul 1, 1865.
Kindig, Jacob, Calumet; discharged Apr 4, 1863; wounds.
Knapp, Isaac W., Calumet; discharged Apr 5, 1863; disability.
Lawler, John W., Calumet; discharged Feb 28, 1863; disability.
Malone, Lawrence, Calumet; deserted Aug 24, 1862.
Maudlin, John, Calumet; discharged May 20, 1865.
McCartney, William S., Calumet; mustered out Jul 1, 1865.
McAvoy, Kern, Calumet; discharged Mar 5, 1863; disability.
McNerny, Michael, Calumet; mustered out Jul 1, 1865.
Murray, John M., Calumet; mustered out.
Murray, Ethan A., Calumet; mustered out.
Munson, Charles, Calumet; died at Silver Springs, TN, Nov 18, 1862.

Osborn, Charles O., Calumet; discharged Apr 20, 1863; disability.
Osborn, Daniel L., Calumet; promoted to Corporal.
Page, William, Calumet; discharged Feb 16, 1864; wounds.
Pendergrast, Thomas, Calumet; deserted Sept 8, 1862.
Peterson, John, Calumet; mustered out.
Piper, James E., Calumet; died at Louisville, Ky, Mar 17, 1863.
Pugh, William H., Calumet; deserted Sept 8, 1862.
Ritter, John J., Calumet; promoted to Corporal.
Samuelson, John P., Calumet; deserted Jun 17, 1863.
Samuelson, Samuel A., Calumet; discharged May 28, 1863; wounds received Dec 31, 1862, Stones River.
Saunders, George L., Calumet; mustered out Jul 1865.
Shuts, Charles, Calumet; mustered out Jul 1, 1865.
Simmons, Henry C., Calumet; mustered out Jul 1, 1865.
Smith, Oscar B., Calumet; discharged Mar 28, 1863; disability.
Smith, James E., Calumet; mustered out Jul 1, 1865.
Smith, Hiram W., Calumet; discharged Oct 5, 1863; wounds.
Spear, Charles S., Calumet; died at Stevenson, Ala., Dec 7, 1864.
Spencer, Orsemus H., Calumet; discharged July 10, 1863; disability.
Stewart, Charles E., Calumet; dishonorably discharged Aug 30, 1864.
Sumner, James B., Calumet; deserted Oct 26, 1862.
Tidball, John W., Calumet; died at Louisville, Ky, Nov 9, 1862.
VanWicklin, Benjamin, Calumet; mustered out Jul 1, 1865.
Vorhes, Benjamin, Calumet; discharged Feb 25, 1863; disability.
Whitmore, Nathan G., Calumet; deserted Apr 30, 1863 in front of enemy.
Wheeler, George, Calumet; discharged Dec 26, 1862; disability.
Wheeler, Elias, Calumet; died at Gallatin, TN, Jan 28,

1863.
Wise, William A., Calumet; discharged Dec 28, 1862; disability.
White, Joseph, Calumet; deserted Aug 18, 1862.
Young, Martin, Calumet; mustered out Jul 1, 1865.

Recruits

Fleeter, Freeborn J., Calumet; transfer 44th Regt Jul 1, 1865.
Johnson, George W., DeKalb County; transfer 44th Regt Jul 1, 1865.
Lord, David, Indianapolis; transfer44th Regt Jul 1, 1865.
Peterson, John A., Calumet; transfer 44th Regt Jul 1, 1865.

Chapter Fifteen

ROSTER, COMPANY F - K

73rd Indiana Volunteer Infantry Regiment

COMPANY F

OFFICERS

Captains

Miles H. Tibbits, Plymouth; Commission Aug 5, 1862; muster Aug 16, 1862; killed in action, Battle of Stones River, TN, Dec 31, 1862.
Matthew Boyd, Plymouth; promoted Captain Dec 3, 1862; resigned Jul 25, 1864.
Horace Gamble, Plymouth; Comm. Jul 26, 1864; muster May 17, 1865; mustered out with regiment.

First Lieutenants

Samuel Wolf, Plymouth; Comm. Aug 5, 1862; muster Aug 16, 1862; resigned Dec 2, 1862.
Matthew Boyd, Plymouth; promoted Captain Dec 3, 1862;
James C. Woodrow, Plymouth; Comm. Jan 2, 1863; muster Feb 17, 1863; promoted Adjutant; mustered out May 15, 1865.
Otto H. Sollan, Plymouth; Comm. Jul 26, 1864; muster Sept 1, 1864; mustered out with regiment.

Second Lieutenants

Matthew Boyd, Plymouth; Comm. Aug 5, 1862; muster Aug 16, 1862; promoted 1st Lieutenant.
Horace Gamble, Plymouth; Comm. Jan 2, 1863; muster Feb 17, 1863; promoted to Captain.
Otto H. Sollan, Plymouth; Comm. May 1, 1864; muster May 25, 1864; promoted 1st Lieutenant.

ENLISTED MEN, COMPANY F

First Sergeants

McDonald, Samuel H., Plymouth; discharged Apr 13, 1863 as private.
Astley, John, Plymouth; mustered out July 1, 1865.

Sergeants

Gamble, Horace, Monroeville, OH; promoted 2nd Lieutenant.
Cummings, James E., Plymouth; mustered out Jul 1, 1865.
Sollan, Otto H., Canal Fulton, OH; promoted 2nd Lieutenant..
Grube, Peter J., Plymouth; mustered out Jul 1, 1865 as private.
Hall, Lyman G., Plymouth; mustered out July 1, 1865.
Whitman, Henry, Bourbon; mustered out Jul 1, 1865.

Corporals

Hall, Lyman G., Plymouth; promoted to Sergeant.
Fife, Samuel B., Tyner City; discharged May 11, 1863; disability.
Matthews, John T., Georgetown, Del; mustered out July 1, 1865.
Astley, John, Plymouth; promoted to 1st Sergeant.
Crandall, Robert, Plymouth; discharged Jul 28, 1863; disability.
Kellog, Thomas O., Ashtabula, OH; died at Gallatin, TN, Jan 21, 1863.
Turner, William, Plymouth; died at Nashville, TN, Jan 18, 1863.
Poulson, George T., Plymouth; mustered out Jul 1, 1865.
Cummins, Marion, Plymouth; mustered out Jul 1, 1865.
Jacobs, Andrew, Tyner City; mustered out July 1, 1865.
Long, David S., Plymouth; mustered out Jul 1, 1865.
Washburn, Isaac W., Plymouth; mustered out Jul 1, 1865.
Yantiss, Joseph, Bourbon; mustered out Jul 1, 1865.

Musicians

Fryer, Samuel, Plymouth; mustered out July 1, 1865.
Ranstead, Leonard H., Plymouth; died at Nashville, TN, Jan 17, 1863.

Wagoner

Jacobs, Peter, Tyner City; discharged Aug 18, 1865; wounds.

Privates

Angerman, William F., Bourbon; mustered out Jul 1, 1865.
Arbaugh, Jacob W., Plymouth; mustered out Jul 1, 1865.
Asper, Abram, Plymouth; died at Columbia, Ky., Oct 17, 1862.
Bochtol, Lewis, Maxinkuckee; mustered out Jul 1, 1865.
Blunk, John H., Tyner City; discharged Oct 23, 1863; disability.
Carr, James H., Plymouth; deserted Sept 26, 1863.
Cochran, Simon, Plymouth; died at Louisville, Ky., Jan 17, 1863.
Clark, Alvin E., Tyner City; discharged Oct 3, 1862; disability.
Cook, Henry S., Plymouth; died at Nashville, TN, Jan 30, 1863.
Crumb, Leander W., Tyner City; mustered out Jul 1, 1865.
Clayton, James, Plymouth; mustered out Jul 1, 1865:
Cummins, Marion, Plymouth; promoted to Corporal.
Delp, John, Guilford, OH mustered out Jul 1, 1865.
Dunham, Ira, Plymouth; died in Louisville, Ky., Jan 21, 1863.
Foot, Adrian V. H., Marmont; discharged Feb 1864; wounds.
Fryer, Robert, Plymouth; mustered out Jul 1, 1865.
Gierent, William, Plymouth; mustered out Jul 1, 1865.
Good, William E., Tyner City ; died at Gallatin, TN, Dec 20, 1862.
Grover, Lewis, Plymouth; died at Nashville, TN, Mar 9, 1863.
Guy, William H., Plymouth; discharged Mar 7, 1863; disability.
Hall, Elias H., Plymouth; discharged Jun 4, 1863; disability.
Hardy, Josiah R., Plymouth; died at Louisville, Ky., Nov 28, 1862.
Harris, Joseph W., Argos; discharged Jan 1, 1863; disability.
Henderson, John, Plymouth; mustered out Jul 1, 1865.
Hildreth, Henry, Plymouth; deserted September 3, 1862.

Hutchinson, John, Plymouth; discharged Mar 25, 1864; disability.
Hume, William C., Plymouth; mustered out Jul 1, 1865.
Inks, John E., Tyner City; transferred to VRC Aug 28, 1863.
Jacobs, Andrew, Tyner City; promoted to Corporal.
Johnson, Howard, Plymouth; died at Nashville, Dec 18, 1862.
Jordan, James, Plymouth; mustered out Jul 1, 1865.
Kayton, Larry, Plymouth; mustered out Jul 1, 1865.
Kelley, Patrick, Bourbon; deserted Sept 10, 1862.
Klingerman, Jesse, Plymouth; discharged Feb 24, 1863; disability.
Lloyd, William H., Plymouth; mustered out Jul 1, 1865.
Long, David S., Plymouth; promoted to Corporal.
Lement, Lewis, mustered out Jul 1, 1865.
Maxey, Jacob, Plymouth; discharged Jun 21, 1865.
McCartney, John, Plymouth; discharged Feb 1, 1863; disability.
Megill, William, Knox; mustered out Jul 1, 1865.
Miller, Amos C., Plymouth; transferred to VRC Oct 30, 1863.
Miller, Eli H., Plymouth; discharged May 26, 1865.
Moore, James M., Plymouth; deserted May 25, 1863.
Moore, George P., Plymouth; discharged May 26, 1865.
Mohler, William H., Plymouth; mustered out Jul 1, 1865.
Mohler, Henry, Plymouth; died at Murfreesboro, TN, Mar 9, 1863.
Morris, John T., Plymouth; died at Nashville, Dec 2, 1862.
Muffley, Jacob, Plymouth; transferred to VRC Dec 20, 1863.
Myers, Mathias, Plymouth; discharged Feb 25, 1863; disability.
Moore, William H., Plymouth; died at New Albany, Ind., Dec 17, 1862.
McCoy, Alexander W., Plymouth; discharged Nov 10, 1862; disability.
Overmier, Harrison, Plymouth; mustered out Jul 1, 1865.
Patterson, John W., Plymouth; mustered out July 1, 1865.
Peck, William M. C., Plymouth; died at Nashville, Dec 23, 1862.
Reynolds, Albert, Plymouth; deserted Nov 4, 1862.
Reynolds, John B., Tyner City; discharged July 11, 1863.
Rhodes, Milton F., Plymouth; died at Nashville, Nov 18, 1862.

Rhodes, Wilber, Plymouth; mustered out Jul 1, 1865.
Roach, Thomas, mustered out Jul 1, 1865.
Robinson, Joseph, South Bend; died at Gallatin, TN, Nov 25, 1862.
Rorick, William, Bourbon; died near South Bend, Aug 19, 1862.
Serrals, Mathew T., Plymouth; died at Nashville, Dec 31, 1862.
Singleton, Benjamin, Tyner City; died at Nashville, Dec 17, 1862.
Singleton, Niles, Tyner City; killed in action at Stones River, Dec 31, 1862.
Stickley, Jonas, Plymouth; discharged Mar 26, 1863; wounds.
Smith, Eli, Plymouth; transferred to VRC Jan 10, 1865.
Spurgeon, Alfred, Plymouth; died at Huntsville, Ala., Feb 16, 1865.
Sweet, Jacob, Plymouth; transferred to VRC Oct 30, 1863.
Stowe, David E., Plymouth; mustered out Jul 1, 1865.
Tippet, Charles W., Plymouth; mustered out Jul 1, 1865.
Thompson, Larkin, Plymouth; deserted Oct 26, 1863.
Vories, Milton M., Plymouth; discharged May 18, 1863; wounds.
Wariner, Gilbert, Plymouth; killed at Stones River Dec 31, 1862.
Washburn, Isaac W., Plymouth; promoted to Corporal.
Washburn, David, Plymouth; mustered out Jul 1, 1865.
Whitsell, John, Plymouth; mustered out Jul 1, 1865.
Whitman, Henry, Bourbon; promoted to Sergeant.
White, Charles E., Rochester; died in rebel prison in Alabama, Nov 4, 1864.
Winget, Josephus, Tyner City; discharged Jun 22, 1863; disability.
Woodrow, James C., Warren, OH; promoted 1st Lieutenant Co F.
Yantiss, Jonah F., Bourbon; died at Nashville, Dec 5, 1862.
Yantiss, Joseph, Bourbon; promoted to Corporal.

Recruits

Bradley, Jacob P., Tyner City; transferred to 29th Regiment Jul 1, 1865.

Bradley, John, Tyner City; transferred to 29th Regiment Jul 1, 1865.

Bradley, Barzali, Tyner City; transferred to 29th Regiment Jul 1, 1865.

Burton, William H., Tyner City; transferred to 29th Regiment Jul 1, 1865.

Bowell, George W., Argos; transferred to 29th Regiment Jul 1, 1865.

Byron, William D., Indianapolis; transferred to 29th Regiment Jul 1, 1865.

Borden, Oliver, Voloney; transferred to 29th Regiment Jul 1, 1865.

Falconburg, James W., Tyner City; transferred to 29th Regiment Jul I, 1865.

Good, John E., Tyner City; transferred to 29th Regiment Jul 1, 1865.

Jenkins, John, Indianapolis; transferred to 29th Regiment Jul I, 1865.

Johnson, Smith, Jeffersonville; transferred to 29th Regiment Jul 1, 1865.

King, Greensburg, Tyner City; transferred to 29th Regiment Jul 1, 1865.

King, Lewis, Tyner City; transferred to 29th Regiment Jul 1, 1865.

Lovell, Sylvester, Tyner City; transferred to 29th Regiment Jul 1, 1865.

Maple, Stephen, Tyner City; transferred to 29th Regiment Jul 1, 1865.

McDaniel, James A., Tyner City; transferred to 29th Regiment Jul 1, 1865.

Price, William, Cincinnati, OH; deserted Apr 27, 1864.

Perry Napoleon, Knoxville; deserted Apr 1, 1864.

Roach, Thomas, Breman; transferred to 29th Regiment Jul 1,1865.

Reprogle, George, Tyner City; transferred to 29th Regiment Jul 1, 1865.

Reprogle, William S., Tyner City; transferred to 29th Regiment July i, 1865.
Reed, David J., Tyner City; transferred to 29th Regiment Jul 1, 1865.
Singleton, George W., Tyner City; transferred to 29th Regiment Jul 1, 1865.
Sumpter, Robert, Tyner City; transferred to 29th Regiment Jul 1, 1865.
Singleton, Charles W., Tyner City; transferred to 29th Regiment Jul 1, 1865.
Shehan, John, Martinsville; transferred to 29th Regiment Jul 1, 1865.
Smithson, Thomas, Middletown; deserted Sept 23, 1863.
Thompson, David, Tyner City; deserted Aug 24, 1863.
Taplin, James, Plymouth; died at Decatur, Ala., Sept 16, 1864.
Walsh, Peter, Plymouth; transferred to 29th Regiment Jul 1, 1865.
Wingeat, Lewis, Tyner City; transferred to 29th Regiment July 1, 1865.
Wiseman, Peter, Plymouth; mustered out May 30, 1865.

COMPANY G

OFFICERS

Captains

McConnell, William L. Logansport; Commission Aug 5, 1862; muster Aug 16, 1862; resigned Feb 6, 1863.
Westlake, Joseph A., Logansport; Comm. Feb 6, 1863; muster Feb 16, 1863; mustered out with regiment.

First Lieutenants

Westlake, Joseph A., Logansport; Comm. Aug 5, 1862; muster Aug 16, 1862; promoted to Captain.
Van Ness, Garrett, A., Logansport; Comm. Feb 16, 1863; muster Feb 17, 1863; mustered out with regiment.

Second Lieutenants

Connelly, Robert J., Logansport; Comm. Aug 5, 1862; muster Aug 16, 1862; mustered out and honorably discharged May 15, 1865; cause, services no longer required and disability.
Wilson, Alexander, Logansport; Comm. Jul 26, 1864; muster Sept 1,1864; mustered out with regiment.
Pratt, Seth B., Logansport; Comm. Jun 20, 1865; mustered out as 1st Sergeant with regiment.

ENLISTED MEN, COMPANY G

First Sergeants

Van Ness, Garrett A., Logansport; promoted 1st Lieutenant.
Pratt, Seth B., Logansport; mustered out with regiment.

Sergeants

Wilson, Alexander, Logansport, promoted 2d Lieutenant; mustered out Jul 1, 1865.
McBane, Gillis G., Logansport; mustered out Jul 1, 1865.

Pawling, Finla, Logansport; mustered out Jul 1, 1865 as private.
McConnell, John, Logansport; mustered out Jul 1, 1865.
Moss, Richard, Logansport; mustered out July 1, 1865.
Sheeder, Isaac, Logansport; mustered out Jul 1, 1865..

Corporals

Banta, Benjamin, Curveton; discharged Feb 1, 1863.
Carnahan, James, Logansport; deserted Oct 7, 1862.
Smith, Lindol, Logansport; transferred VRC Jan 14, 1864.
Moss, Richard, Logansport; promoted to Sergeant.
Sheeder, Isaac, Logansport; promoted to Sergeant.
Lucas, Edward, Logansport; died at Nashville, TN, May 12, 1863.
Kimball, James P., Logansport; deserted Aug 23, 1862.
McDonough, William, Logansport; died Feb 9, 1863; wounds, Stones River.
Burton, Hezekiah, Logansport; mustered out Jul 1, 1865.
Eurite, Decatur H., Logansport; mustered out Jul 1, 1865.
Foust, William, Logansport; mustered out Jul 1, 1865.
Hart, Silas W., Logansport; mustered out Jul 1, 1865.

Musicians

Smith, William H. H., Logansport; mustered out Jul 1, 1865.
Pryor, David E., Logansport; discharged; wounds.

Wagoner

Fox, Jonathan, Logansport; discharged; disability.

Privates

Anderson, John K., Logansport; died at Glasgow, Ky, Nov 3, 1862.
Antrim, James T., Logansport; died at Gallatin, TN, Jan 5, 1863.
Arthurhults, Samuel, Logansport; discharged Jan 23, 1863.
Bennett, Lewis H., Logansport; died at Huntsville, Ala., Feb 24, 1864.
Bennett, William H., Logansport; mustered out Jul 1, 1865.
Binney, Isaac L., Logansport; killed near Bellepont, Ala., Apr 25, 1865.

Boozer, Peter, Logansport; died at Nashville, TN, Jan 3, 1863.
Burton, Hezekiah, Logansport; promoted to Corporal.
Caulfield, John, Logansport; discharged Feb 19, 1863.
Chalk, John, Logansport; discharged Mar 5, 1863.
Clark, Milo, Logansport; deserted Mar 1, 1863.
Corcoran, William, Logansport; mustered out Jul 1, 1865.
Corey, Isaac N., Logansport; discharged Mar 2, 1863.
Crisler, John W., Logansport; mustered out Jul 1, 1865.
Dangerfield, Benjamin F., Logansport; killed near Bellepont, Ala., Apr 25, 1865.
Davis, William, Logansport; died at Nashville, TN, Jan 11, 1863.
Downs, William H., Logansport; mustered out Jul 1, 1865.
Droke, Job K., Logansport; mustered out Jul 1, 1865.
Dugan, Lewis F., Logansport; died at Paducah, Ky., May 9, 1863.
Etmeir, William M., Logansport; died Mar 23, 1863; wounds.
Eurite, Decatur H., Logansport; promoted to Corporal.
Faurote, Abraham, Logansport; discharged Feb 1863.
Fisher, Andrew B., Logansport; discharged Jul 31, 1863.
Foust, William, Logansport; promoted to Corporal.
Glency, Patrick, Logansport; deserted Mar 1, 1863.
Gorden, William, Logansport; died at Bowling Green, Ky., Nov 23, 1862.
Gugal, Christian, Logansport; mustered out Jul 1, 1865.
Gugal, William, Logansport; mustered out Jul 1, 1865.
Hamerly, William, Logansport; mustered out Jul 1, 1865.
Hart, Silas W., Logansport; promoted to Corporal.
Hess, Samuel C., Logansport; died at Silver Springs, TN, Nov 17, 1862.
Helm, Francis M., Logansport; discharged Feb 4, 1863.
Highman, Tilghman M., Logansport; died at Louisville, Ky, Nov 1, 1862.
Jacks, William H., Logansport; mustered out Jul 1, 1865.
Johnson, Anthony S., Logansport; died at Louisville, Ky, Nov 3, 1862.
Johnson, Patrick C., Logansport; mustered out Jul 1, 1865.
Kemp, Allen W., Logansport; mustered out Jul 1, 1865.
Keis, John, Logansport; discharged Mar 2, 1863; wounds.

Kirkman, William G., Logansport; discharged Dec 10, 1862.
Ladd, Christopher M., Logansport; deserted Mar 7, 1863.
Lawrence, Francis M., Logansport; mustered out Jul 1, 1865.
Lawrence, Harrison, Logansport; died at Quincy, Ill., Mar 13, 1863.
Lavell, Francis M., Logansport; mustered out Jul 1, 1865.
McGraugh, Simon, Logansport; discharged Dec 10, 1862.
McMasters, Robert B., Logansport; discharged Jan 8, 1865.
Michael, George, Logansport; mustered out Jul 1, 1865.
Miller, Charles E., Logansport; died at Bowling Green: Ky, Nov 29, 1862.
Nuff, Beman, Logansport; discharged Dec 1, 1862.
Nuff, Daniel, Logansport; discharged Feb 4, 1863.
Oliver, Joseph, Logansport ; mustered out Jul 1, 1865.
Palmer, John N., Logansport; died at Nashville, TN, Dec 19, 1862.
Patterson, Alexander D., Logansport; mustered out Jul 1, 1865.
Penny, Noah R., Logansport; discharged May 24, 1865.
Perry, Reuben, Logansport; died at Logansport, Ind., Dec 7, 1862.
Perry, William, Logansport; mustered out Jul 1, 1865.
Petty, Augustus W., Logansport; deserted Mar 1, 1863.
Poff, William, Logansport; died at Louisville, Ky, April 30, 1863.
Powell, Ephraim, Logansport; killed in action, Stones River, Dec 31, 1862.
Pratt, Seth B., Logansport; promoted to 1st Sergeant.
Rader, Lewis, Logansport; deserted Jun 20, 1863.
Richardson, Archibald, Logansport; discharged Mar 4, 1863.
Ring, Michael, Logansport; mustered out Jul 1, 1865.
Roherberry, Henry. G., Logansport; died at Bowling Green, Ky, Dec 1, 1862.
Rist, Harrison C., Logansport; deserted Sept 11, 1862.
Rouse, John L., Logansport; died at Annapolis, Md, Jul 1, 1863.
Scully, Edward, Logansport; died at Louisville, Ky.
Searight, William, Logansport; mustered out Jul 1, 1865.
Shepherd William, Logansport; discharged Feb 26, 1863.
Smith, George H., Logansport; mustered out Jul 1, 1865.
Smith, Hiram, Logansport; mustered out Jul 1, 1865.
Surface, Flavius S. T., Logansport; mustered out Jul 1, 1865.

Thayer, John J., Logansport; transferred U. S. Marines Mar 1, 1863.
Vanscoyk, Elam, Logansport; mustered out Jul 1, 1865.
Vestal, Lafayette, Logansport; discharged Oct 2, 1862.
Walters, John S., Logansport; discharged Mar, 1863.
Watts, William H., Logansport; discharged Apr 23, 1865.
Weaver, Jehu P., Logansport; discharged Feb 4, 1863.
Weaver, Thomas F., Logansport; discharged Dec 11, 1862.
Winters, John F., Logansport; died of wounds received at Blount's Farm, Ala.
Wolford, George, Logansport; discharged Feb 1, 1863.
Worley, Bartholomew, Logansport; transferred U. S. Marines Mar 1, 1863.
Zerfice, Ambrose, Logansport; transferred VRC Jan 3, 1864.

Recruits

Bennett, John L., died at Huntsville, Ala., Apr 24, 1865.
Bennett, Thomas J., died at Decatur, Ala., Apr 1864.
Barnum, Josiah B., transferred to 29th Regt Jul 1, 1865.
Cost, John W., transferred to 29th Regt Jul 1, 1865.
Coulson, Edward R.; transferred to 29th Regt Jul 1, 1865.
Curtner, Beneville S., transferred to 29th Regt Jul 1, 865.
Cranmore, Gilbert, died at Pulaski, TN, Sept 17, 1864.
Faust, Lewis C., transferred to 29th Regt Jul 1, 1865.
Fordyce, William H., transferred to 29th Regt Jul 1, 1865.
Hipple, Isaac J., transferred to 29th Regt Jul 1, 1865.
Hassich, Christian, died in hospital in Alabama, Jun 24, 1864.
Jordan, Hugh A., mustered out Aug 3, 1865.
Langton, David W., discharged Apr 20, 1863.
Lohman, Daniel, transferred to 29th Regt Jul 1,1865.
Lodge, Horatio, mustered out Jul 24, 1865.
Morrison, David A., transferred to 29th Regt Jul 1, 1865.
Pollard, Adam C., transferred to 29th Regt Jul 1, 1865.
Pierce, Michael, transferred to 29th Regt Jul 1, 1865.
Steward, Charles R., transferred to 29th Regt Jul 1, 1865.
Tippett, Eli, transferred to 29th Regt Jul 1, 1865.
Ward, Joshua B., transferred to 29th Regt Jul 1, 1865.
Williams, Benjamin, transferred to 29th Regt Jul 1, 1865.
Weaver, William, transferred to 29th Regt Jul 1, 1865.

Weaver, John J., transferred to 29th Regt Jul 1, 1865.
Zanna, George W., transferred to 29th Regt Jul 1, 1865.

COMPANY H

OFFICERS

Captains

Doyle, Peter, Logansport; Commission Aug 5, 1862; muster Aug 16, 1862; killed in action at Stones River, TN, Dec 31, 1862.
Mull, Daniel H., Logansport; Comm. Jan 2, 1863; muster Feb 16, 1863; mustered out with regiment.

First Lieutenants

Mull, Daniel H., Logansport; Comm. Aug 5, 1862; muster Aug 16, 1862; promoted to Captain.
Murdock, Henry S., Logansport; Comm. Jan 2, 1863; muster Feb 17, 1863; mustered out with regiment.

Second Lieutenants

Callahan, Andrew M., Logansport; Comm. Aug 5, 1862; muster Aug 16, 1862; mustered out and honorably discharged May 15, 1865; cause, services no longer required, and disability from wounds.
Dailey, Willson, Kokomo; promoted from Sergeant.

ENLISTED MEN, COMPANY H

First Sergeants

Murdock, Henry S., Logansport; promoted 1st Lieutenant.
Merrell, Villars, Jr., Auburn, N. Y; mustered out Jul 1, 1865.

Sergeants

Thornton, Henry H., Kokomo; killed at Stones River, Dec 31, 1862.
Merrell, Villars, Jr., Auburn, N. Y; promoted to 1st Sgt.
Custer, George B., Logansport; mustered out Jul 1, 1865.
Dailey, Willson, Kokomo; promoted to 2d Lieutenant.
Freeman, David O., Kokomo; mustered out Jul 1, 1865.

Hensley, Daniel, Logansport; mustered out Jul 1, 1865.

Corporals

Freeman, David O., Kokomo; promoted to Sergeant.
Sergeant, Leander B., Logansport; discharged Oct 12, 1863; wounds.
Hoffman, Andrew J., New Waverly; mustered out July 1, 1865.
Moore, Anson E., Springfield, OH.; mustered out Jul 1, 1865.
Clement, Charles, Galveston; mustered out Jul 1, 1865.
Hensley, Daniel, Logansport; promoted to Sergeant.
Harwood, Ebenezer, Logansport; died at Nashville, Dec 10, 1862.
Bell, Nathaniel, Logansport; discharged Feb 4, 1863; disability.
Fry, Martin, Logansport; mustered out Jul 1, 1865.
Guthridge, Thomas W., New London; mustered out Jul 1, 1865.
Reeves, Homer J. C., Plymouth; mustered out Jul 1, 1865.

Musicians

Callahan, John F., Logansport; discharged Dec 26, 1862; disability.
Pierce, Robert R. R., Galveston; mustered out Jul 1, 1865.

Wagoner

Morrison, John B., Logansport; discharged Mar 5, 1863; disability.

Privates

Ball, William P., Lafayette; mustered out Jul 1, 1865.
Blackburn, Joseph, Logansport; died at Perryville, Ky., Oct 13, 1862.
Boothe, Wilson, Logansport; discharged Apr 9, 1863; disability.
Brown, Edward, Galveston; mustered out Jul 1, 1865.
Burns, Samuel, Logansport; killed in action, Stones River, Dec 31, 1862.
Campbell, Robert B., Logansport; deserted Aug 29, 1862.
Cantner, Joseph, Rockfield; mustered out Jul 1, 1865.
Chesnut, Samuel, Logansport; died at Nashville, Dec 26, 1862.
Clark, Henry A., Galveston; discharged Feb 1, 1863; disability.
Clement, Charles, Galveston; promoted to Corporal.
Conner, John H. D., Walton; mustered out Jul 1, 1865.

Cook, Corydon W., Galveston; mustered out Jul 1, 1865.
Corning, Hiram V. N., Loudonville, OH; mustered out Jul 1, 1865.
Cottrall, Jefferson, Walton; mustered out Jul 1, 1865.
Crain, John, Logansport; died at Gallatin, TN, Jun 12, 1863.
Crain, Jesse, Logansport; discharged Sept 19, 1863; disability.
Crawford, Robert, Royal Centre; discharged Feb 2, 1863; disability.
Donnally, James E., deserted Oct 19, 1863.
Doud, Wilber, Star City; died at Nashville, Nov 21, 1862.
Enyart, Martin V., Logansport; mustered out Jul 1, 1865.
Fallis, John W., Star City; discharged Jun 5, 1863; disability.
Fiddler, John H., Walton; killed in action, Stones River Dec 31, 1862.
Foy, Reuben, Galveston; died at Nashville, Nov 22, 1862.
Glidden, Henry H., Logansport; mustered out Jul 1, 1865.
Guthridge, Thomas W., New London; promoted to Corporal.
Harbert, Franklin, Galveston; discharged Dec 18, 1862; disability.
Haworth, Daniel, Galveston; mustered out Jul 1, 1865.
Healey, Abner, Logansport; died Jan 17, 1863; wounds received at Stones River.
Hensley, James, Logansport; mustered out Jul 1, 1865.
Henderson, James, Logansport; died at Indianapolis, Sept 4, 1863.
Herd, Thomas, Logansport; transferred to VRC Apr 1, 1865.
Hollenback, Zimri, Logansport; discharged Mar 5, 1863; disability.
Hood, John T., Peru; mustered out Jul 1, 1865.
Horn, Jonathan, Blue Grass; discharged Feb 16, 1863; disability.
Howard, John, Logansport; died, Gallatin, TN, Jan 29, 1863.
Hubbard, George M., Richmond; discharged for promotion Oct 24, 1863; promoted 1st Lieutenant and Regimental Quartermaster.
Jenners, Chesley, Clermont, Iowa; mustered out Jul 1, 1865.
Johnson, Edward, Logansport; discharged Jan 12, 1864; disability.
John, George A., Logansport; transferred to VRC Nov 31, 1863.
Julian, Nathan J., Logansport; died at Silver Springs, TN, Nov 18, 1862.

Julian, William J., Logansport; mustered out Jul 1, 1865.
Kearns, James, Logansport; mustered out Jul 1, 1865.
Kilmer, Christian, Mishawaka; discharged Apr 8, 1863; wounds.
Klopp, Henry, Logansport; discharged Aug 20, 1864; disability.
Knight, Cornelius H., Walton; mustered out Jul 1, 1865.
Loman, George, Logansport; discharged Jan 20, 1863.
Mader Daniel, Logansport; discharged Feb 12, 1863; disability.
Mahaffie, John, Logansport; died at Gallatin, TN, Jan 20, 1863.
Malaby, Thomas A., Lincoln; discharged Feb 22, 1863; disability.
Martin, John A., Logansport; mustered out Jul 1, 1865.
Mason, Thomas R., Richmond; mustered out Jul 1, 1865.
Miller, James, Royal Centre; mustered out Jul 1, 1865.
Morgan, Nathan B., Logansport; mustered out Jul 1, 1865.
McElwain, James F., Galveston; mustered out Jul 1, 1865.
McElwain, Oscar, Galveston; discharged Mar 28, 1863; disability.
McConnell, James H., Bennett Station; mustered out Jul 1, 1865.
Murphy, John, Logansport; mustered out Jul 1, 1865.
Overson, Linzey, Carsville; died at Nashville, Jul 3, 1863.
Ogburn, Calvin, Galveston; deserted.
Paton, John J., Blue Grass; mustered out Jul 1, 1865.
Pierson, Joseph, New Waverly; died at Silver Springs, TN, Nov 20, 1862.
Reeves, Homer J. C., Plymouth; promoted to Corporal.
Sanderson, Adam E., Logansport; discharged Mar 12, 1863; wounds.
Shanton, Edward D., Coshocton, OH; mustered out Jul 1, 1865.
Shilling, Simon K., Logansport; deserted.
Shields, Joshua, Logansport; missing in action, Stones River, Dec 31, 1862.
Stanford, John, Logansport; mustered out Jul 1, 1865.
Stallard, William D., Logansport; discharged Nov 22, 1862; disability.
Stevens, William, Logansport; discharged Jan 25, 1863; disability.
Thompson, John M., Logansport; mustered out Jul 1, 1865.
Turflinger, Benjamin F., Galveston; died at Gallatin, TN, Feb 2,

1863.
Tyson, Thornton, New Waverly; discharged Mar 31, 1863; disability.
Wallace, William B., Rochester; died at Camp Dennison, OH, Mar 5, 1863.
Warfield, George A., Logansport; mustered out Jul 1, 1865.
Warfield, Elijah J., Logansport; mustered out Jul 1, 1865.
Ward, William H. H., Logansport; discharged Nov 30, 1862; disability.
Weaver, Charles F., Logansport; mustered out Jul 1, 1865.
West, Charles H., Logansport; transferred to VRC Nov 3, 1863.
Williamson, Edward, Logansport; missing in action, Stones River, Dec 31, 1862.
Wolfkill, Alfred, Logansport; died at Louisville, Ky., Jan 20, 1863.
Yeates, Isaac B., Logansport; mustered out Jul 1, 1865.
York, James, Mexico; mustered out Jul 1, 1865.

Recruits

Davidson, William H., Logansport; transfer to 29th Regt. Jul 1, 1865.
Enyart, William B., Logansport; transfer to 29th Regt. Jul 1, 1865.
Ferrell, Henry, Mexico; transfer to 29th Regt. Jul 1, 1865.
Livingston, William, Logansport; transfer to 29th Regt. Jul 1, 1865.
Michaels, Charles, Logansport; transfer to 29th Regt. Jul 1, 1865.
Stallard, William D., Logansport; transfer to 29th Regt. Jul 1, 1865.
Spiker, William R., Logansport; transfer to 29th Regt. Jul 1, 1865.
Welk, Julius A., Logansport; transfer to 29th Regt. Jul 1, 1865.

COMPANY I

OFFICERS

Captains

Pratt, Rollin M., Valparaiso; Commission dated Aug 5, 1862; muster Aug 16, 1862; resigned Oct 19, 1862.
Graham, Robert W., Valparaiso; Comm. Oct 20, 1862; muster Oct 20, 1862; promoted Lieutenant-Colonel.
Williamson, Emanuel M., Valparaiso; Comm. Feb 13, 1863; muster Feb 16, 1863; discharged by order of the Secretary of War, Feb 15, 1864.
Eaton, William C., Valparaiso; Comm. Mar 1, 1864; muster Jun 7, 1864; mustered out with regiment.
Stoddard, Lewis S., Tassinong; promoted from Pvt. to Captain Commanding 12th U. S. Colored Troops.

First Lieutenants

Graham, Robert W., Valparaiso; Comm. Aug 5, 1862; muster Aug 16, 1862; promoted Captain.
Williamson, Emanuel M., Valparaiso; Comm. Oct 20, 1862; muster Oct 20, 1862; promoted Captain.
Eaton, William C., Valparaiso; Comm. Feb 13, 1863; muster Feb 16, 1863; promoted Captain.
Booher, Adolphus H., Valparaiso; Comm. Mar 1, 1864; mustered out as 2nd Lieutenant with regiment.

Second Lieutenants

Williamson, Emanuel M. Valparaiso; Comm. Aug 5, 1862; muster Aug 16, 1862; promoted 1st Lieutenant.
Eaton, William C., Valparaiso; Comm. Oct 20, 1862; muster Nov 2, 1862; promoted 1st Lieutenant.
Booher, Adolphus H., Valparaiso ; Comm. Feb 13, 1863; muster Apr 10, 1863; promoted from Pvt. to 1st Lieutenant.
Arnold, Charles S., Valparaiso; Comm. Mar 1, 1864; muster Sept 1,1864; mustered out and honorably discharged as supernumerary.

Arnold, Charles S., Wheeler; promoted from Private.

ENLISTED MEN, COMPANY I

First Sergeants

Eaton, William C., Valparaiso; promoted 2nd Lieutenant.
Kersey, Robert B., Wheeler; promoted from Pvt.; mustered out Jul 1, 1865.

Sergeants

Witham, Simon, Valparaiso; discharged Oct 2, 1862; wounds.
Hendee, William H., Tassinong; killed in action, Stones River, Dec 31, 1862.
Stroud, Thomas, Wheeler Station; transfer to VRC Jan 15, 1863.
Clark, Thomas, Crown Point; discharged Feb I, 1863; disability.
Maxwell, John, Tassinong; mustered out Jul 1, 1865.
Jaqua, Uriah D., Lowell; mustered out Jul 1, 1865.
Harding, Stephen D., Valparaiso; mustered out July 1, 1865.
Stallcup, Benjamin, Wheeler; mustered out Jul 1, 1865.

Corporals

Maxwell, John, Tassinong; promoted to Sergeant.
Cowley, Scott E., Tassinong; mustered out Jul 1, 1865.
Purday, Thomas S., Valparaiso; discharged Mar 27, 1863; wounds.
Bair, Benjamin F., Valparaiso; discharged Mar 21, 1863; disability.
Watson, Wesley M., Wheeler Station; died at Danville, Ky., Oct 19, 1862.
Bradley, George J., Valparaiso; died at Nashville, Dec 5, 1862.
Graves, Elijah, Valparaiso; mustered out Jul 1, 1865.
Jaqua, Uriah D., Lowell; promoted to Sergeant.
Baughman, Thomas J., Lowell; mustered out Jul 1, 1865.
Brother of Pvt. Wilson Shannon Baughman, Co. A.
Kersey, Albert H., Wheeler; mustered out Jul 1, 1865.

Muscians

Hunter, George W., Wheeler; discharged Jan 16, 1863; disability.
Spinner, William, Valparaiso; mustered out May 15, 1865.
Willey, Joseph H., Wheeler; mustered out Jul 1, 1865.

Wagoner

Spray, Banister, Wheeler; discharged Dec 19, 1862; disability.

Privates

Adams, Henry W., Deep River; died of wounds received at Stones River.
Alyea, Jacob, Hebron; discharged Feb 5, 1863; disability.
Arnold, Charles S., Wheeler; promoted to 2nd Lieutenant.
Asher, Edward, Tassinong; mustered out Jul 1, 1865.
Asher, John, Tassinong; discharged Mar 19, 1863; disability.
Asher, John I., Tassinong; discharged Oct 10, 1863; wounds.
Barnes, George W., Valparaiso; deserted Oct 7, 1863.
Baughman, Thomas J., Lowell; promoted to Corporal; brother of Pvt. Wilson Shannon Baughman, Co. A.
Blackley, Napolean B., Wheeler; died at Silver Springs, Nov 16, 1862.
Booher, Adolphus H., Westville; promoted to 2nd Lieutenant.
Brown, William V., Tassinong; discharged Feb 3, 1863; disability.
Brown, John, Lowell; killed in action, Stones River, Dec 31, 1862.
Cain, William, Valparaiso; discharged Dec 19, 1862; disability.
Cavilee, Philander, Valparaiso; deserted Oct 1, 1862.
Clifford, Daniel S., Wheeler; discharged Mar 1, 1863; disability.
Comer, Samuel, Valparaiso; died at Summersville, Ky., May 25, 1863.
Crisman, Harrison, Wheeler; mustered out Jul 1, 1865.
Crisman, William, Wheeler; died at Nashville, TN, Dec 29, 1863.
Curtis, Alanthus, Wheeler; transfer VRC Jul 15, 1863.
Curtis, Horace H., Wanatah ; killed in action, Stones River, Dec 31, 1862.

Cross, William, Lowell; deserted Oct 27, 1862.
Cushman, Thomas W., Lowell; discharged May 15, 1863; disability.
Dodd, William H. H., West Creek; died at Lebanon, Ky., Dec 1, 1862.
Dorcey, Curtis, Valparaiso; died at Nashville, TN, Nov 28, 1862.
Evenes, Robert O., Tassinong; discharged Mar 3, 1863; disability.
Flewellen, Robert, Wheeler; killed in action at Decatur, Ala., Oct 27, 1864.
Flewellen, Isaac, Wheeler; mustered out Jul 1, 1865.
Fuller, Joseph A., Wheeler; discharged Mar 7, 1863; disability.
Gordon, Eli J., Wheeler; discharged Oct 9, 1864; disability.
Hall, Theodore R., Tassinong; died at Camp Chase, OH, Jun 8, 1863.
Hann, Eli E., North Judson; mustered out Jul 1, 1865.
Hankins, John, Tassinong; died at Lebanon, Ky., Oct 29, 1862.
Harding, Stephen D., Valparaiso; promoted to Sergeant.
Hoch, Jacob, Wanatah; died at Nashville, TN, Nov 28, 1862.
Hooseline, Michael, Wheeler; mustered out Jul 1, 1865.
Iseminger, William, Tassinong; mustered out Jul 1, 1865.
Julian, Miller, Tassinong; discharged Jun 19, 1863; disability.
Kanarr, Charles C., Cedar Lake; discharged Dec 28, 1862; accidental wounds.
Kennedy, Edwin A., Wheeler; mustered out May 17, 1865.
Kersey, Albert H., Wheeler; promoted to Corporal.
Kersey, Robert B., Wheeler; promoted to 1st Sergeant.
Kouts, Daniel, Tassinong; died Jan 18, 1863; wounds.
Kouts, Samuel G., Tassinong; discharged March 31, 1863; disability.
Lane, John C., North Judson; discharged March 16, 1863; wounds.
Lansing, Robert, Valparaiso; discharged Feb 5, 1863; disability.
Libby, William, Wheeler; mustered out Jul 1, 1865.
Long, Jeremiah A., Wanatah; mustered out Jul 1, 1865.
Maine, David G., Tassinong; died at Nashville, TN, Nov 30, 1862.
Marsh, Harlow, Valparaiso; died at Danville, Ky., May 15, 1863.
McCumsey, Jacob, Wanatah; mustered out Jul 1, 1865.
McCurday, George, Tassinong; killed in action, Stones River, Dec 31, 1862,

Milner, George S., Wheeler; mustered out Jul 1, 1865.
Maxwell, George, Tassinong; mustered out Jul 1, 1865.
Nalley, Sebastian, Westville; died at Tuscumbia, Ala., Apr 30, 1863.
Neff, Joseph, Wheeler; discharged Jun 19, 1863; disability.
Nickerson, Alexander, Tassinong; discharged Feb 23, 1863; disability.
Phillips, Norton J., Lowell; transfer to VRC Dec 29, 1863.
Reed, James H., Westville; discharged Jul 31, 1863; wounds.
Sanders, Horace, Lowell; died, Murfreesboro, Mar 18, 1863.
Sherman, Amasa, Valparaiso; discharged Dec 19, 1862; disability.
Shull, Thomas C., Wheeler; killed in action, Stones River, Dec 31, 1862.
Shull, Edward, Wheeler, discharged Oct 3, 1863; disability.
Smith, Alexander, Wheeler; died at Murfreesboro, Jul 23, 1863.
Smith, Lewis, Valparaiso; discharged Feb 22, 1863; disability.
Spencer, Albert, Tassinong; discharged May 18, 1863; disability.
Stinchcomb, Charles, Valparaiso; killed in action, Stones River, Dec 31, 1862.
Stallcup, Benjamin, Wheeler; promoted to Sergeant.
Stoddard, John, Tassinong; mustered out July 1, 1865.
Stoddard, Lewis S., Tassinong; promoted to Captain 12th U. S. Colored Troops.
Sturdevant, Solomon, Wheeler; mustered out Jul 1, 1865.
Surprise, Harvey, Lowell; mustered out July 1, 1865.
Squire, Edwin S., Valparaiso; died at Danville, Ky., Oct 20, 1862.
Thornton, Stephen, Valparaiso; died in hospital, Jan 24, 1865.
Trinkle, Leander, Tassinong; transfer to VRC Oct 30, 1863.
Underwood, William H., Wheeler; died at Nashville, Dec 19, 1862.
Wallace, Frank W., Wheeler; transfer to VRC Oct 30, 1863.
Walton, Hiram W., Wheeler; died at Nashville, TN, Feb 19, 1863.
Webb, Delarma, Tassinong; mustered out Jul 1, 1865.
Willey, Joseph H., Wheeler; promoted to Corporal.
Williamson, William J., Tassinong; mustered out Jul 1, 1865.

Woods, Charles, Deep River; discharged Mar 1, 1863; disability.
Wright, Richard W., Merrillville; mustered out Jul 1, 1865.

Recruits

Asher, John, Wheeler; transfer to 29th Regt. Jul 1, 1865.
Cassity, Charles, Boston; transfer to 29th Regt. July l, 1865.
Conley, John, deserted Oct 3, 1862.
Schofield, John F., Lake Co; transfer to 29th Regt. Jul 1,1865.
Underwood, James H., Wheeler; transfer to 29th Regt. Jul 1, 1865.

COMPANY K

OFFICERS

Captains

WALKER, IVAN N., Michigan City; Commission Aug 5, 1862; muster Aug 16, 1862; promoted to Major.
Phelps, Ithamer D., Michigan City; Comm. Feb 13, 1863; muster Feb 18, 1863; mustered out with regiment.

First Lieutenants

Phelps, Ithamer D., Michigan City; Comm. Aug, 1862; muster Aug 16, 1862; promoted to Captain.
Reynolds, Williams, Westville; Comm. Feb 13, 1863; muster Feb 18, 1863; resigned Jul 23, 1864; wounds at battle of Stones River.
Williams, Leander P., Westville; Comm. Jul 24, 1864; muster Sept 1, 1864; mustered out with regiment.

Second Lieutenants

Butterfield, John, Cool Spring; Comm. Aug 5, 1862; muster Aug 16, 1862; resigned Jan 9, 1863.
Leander P. Williams, Westville; Comm. Feb 13, 1863; muster March 1, 1863; promoted to 1st Lieutenant.
Dailey, Wilson, Kokomo; Comm. Jul 24, 1864; muster Sept 1, 1864; promoted from 1st Sergeant Company H; mustered out with regiment.1865.
Cassity, Charles, Boston; transfer to 29th Regt. Jul 1, 1865.
Conley, John, deserted Oct 3, 1862.
Schofield, John F., Lake Co.; transfer to 29th Regt. Jul 1, 1865.
Underwood, James H.Wheeler; transfer to 29th Regt. July 1, 1865.

ENLISTED MEN, COMPANY K

First Sergeants

Reynolds, William, Westville; promoted to 1st Lieutenant.
Barnard, Job, Westville; mustered out Jul 1, 1865.

Sergeants

Fairchild, Ezra, Michigan City; transferred VRC Oct 4, 1863.
Harding, Benjamin, Michigan City; discharged May 20, 1863.
Reynolds, Silas H., Westville; discharged May 15, 1865.
Denny, Joseph, Crossing; mustered out Jul 1, 1865.
Kilburn, Henry, Michigan City; mustered out Jul 1, 1865.
Myers, Frederick, Michigan City; mustered out July 1, 1865.
Williams, John M., Westville; mustered out July 1, 1865.

Corporals

Halliday, William, Westville; discharged Apr 3, 1863.
Weston, Carey I., Crossing; killed in action, Stones River, Dec 31, 1862.
Hammond, John E., Westville; transfer to Mississippi. Marine Brigade, Mar 25, 1863.
Beatty, Sidney, Crossing; mustered out Jul 1, 1865.
Kilburn, Henry, Michigan City; promoted to Sergeant.
Clark, Jonathan D., Westville; died, Huntsville, Ala., Nov 26, 1864.
Culver, John A., Crossing; died at Nashville, TN, Dec 12, 1862.
Linza, Andrew J., Westville; mustered out Jul 1, 1865.
Boothe, George, Crossing; mustered out July 1, 1865. Friend of Pvt. Hiram S. Root.
Deeds, Leroy, Michigan City; mustered out Jul 1, 1865.
Donaldson, William, Westville; mustered out Jul 1, 1865.
Ferris, James J., Westville; discharged Oct 19, 1863; wounds.
Reynolds, John N., Crossing; mustered out Jul 1, 1865.
Webster, Amos G., Westville; mustered out Jul 1, 1865.
Williams, Harrison H., Westville; mustered out July 1, 1865.

Musicians

Swinney, Charles, Michigan City; killed at Perryville, Ky., Oct 8, 1862.
Jernegan, Edward A., Michigan City; discharged Mar 19, 1863.

Wagoner

Peck, Miles W., Michigan City; killed in action Stones River.

Privates

Allen, Hiram F., Michigan City; died at Silver Springs, Nov 19, 1862.
Augustine, Christian, Westville; killed in action, Stones River, Dec 31, 1862.
Bales, Thomas C., Westville; mustered out Jul 1, 1865.
Barnard, Job, Westville; promoted to 1st Sergeant.
Behan, Robert, Michigan City; mustered out Jul 1, 1865.
Bennett, Hiram H., Westville; discharged Mar 2, 1863.
Bird, Henry, Michigan City; missing at the Battle of Day's Gap, Ala., April 30, 1863.
Boothe, George, Crossing; promoted to Corporal. Friend of Pvt Hiram S. Root.
Bowen, James, Westville; discharged Jun 5, 1865; wounds.
Cape, James, Westville; discharged Mar 2, 1863.
Carr, Shannon, Crossing; missing at the Battle of Day's Gap, Ala., April 30, 1863.
Clement, William H., New Durham; mustered out Jul 1, 1865.
Corser, True, Crossing; died at Nashville, TN, Dec 14, 1862.
Corser, Anthony B., Crossing; died at Gallatin, TN, Jan 8, 1863.
Deeds, Leroy, Michigan City; promoted to Corporal.
Doing, Charles H., Westville; mustered out Jul 1, 1865.
Doing, James R., Westville; discharged Oct 29, 1863.
Donaldson, William, Westville; promoted to Corporal.
Donnell, William, Michigan City; mustered out Jul 1, 1865.
Donnell, Joseph, Michigan City; died at Nashville, Dec 6, 1862.
Ferris, James J., Westville; promoted to Corporal.
Gibson, John W., Westville; discharged Dec 29, 1862.
Goodwin, Clayton S., Crossing; discharged Aug 11, 1863; wounds.

Gordon, Galathia, Michigan City; mustered out Jul 1, 1865.
Hagherty, Timothy, South Bend; deserted Aug 20, 1862.
Halladay, John G., Westville; discharged Feb 16, 1863.
Hammond, James R., Michigan City; discharged Feb 21,1863.
Harsfield, James, Michigan City; mustered out Jul 1, 1865.
Hart, Franklin N., Michigan City; mustered out Jul 1, 1865.
Haskin, Abner S., Walkerton; mustered out Jul 1, 1865.
Herrington, Henry B., Michigan City; discharged Dec 20, 1862.
Herrold, John, Crossing; mustered out July 1, 1865.
Houston, Rufus, Crossing; died at Danville, Ky., Oct 24, 1862.
Houston, John, Michigan City; mustered out Jul 1, 1865.
Howard, Thomas, Michigan City; mustered out Jul 1, 1865.
Jacobus, John G., Michigan City; discharged Jan 21, 1863.
Jackson, Joseph C., Calumet; mustered out Jul 1, 1865.
Jackson, Charles D., Calumet; mustered out Jul 1, 1865.
Kettle, James J., Westville; discharged Feb 18, 1863.
Maulsby, Clark F., Westville; died at Nashville, Jan 12, 1863.
McAulife, Michael, Michigan City; mustered out Jul 1, 1865.
McFadden, Angus, Michigan City; discharged Jun 10, 1865.
McNally, James, Valparaiso; killed in action, Stones River, Dec 31, 1862.
McNeal, Joseph, Michigan City; discharged Aug 25, 1862.
Miller, Hiram W., Valparaiso; mustered out Jul 1, 1865.
Myers, Charles, Michigan City; mustered out Jul 1, 1865.
Myers, Frederick, Michigan City; promoted to Sergeant.
Neville, John, Crossing; mustered out Jul 1, 1865.
Perly, George, Michigan City; mustered out Jul 1, 1865.
Petro, John M., Westville; mustered out Jul 1, 1865.
Petersdorf, Julius, Michigan City; deserted Jun 15, 1863.
Petersdorf, Franklin, Cool Spring; deserted Nov 4, 1862.
Peterson, William H., New Durham; killed in action, Stones River, Dec 31, 1862.
Quinn, Michael, Michigan City; discharged Feb 27, 1864.
Quirk, Thomas, Michigan City; missing in action at Lexington, Ky., Sept 1, 1862.
Reed, James V., Westville; discharged Feb 18, 1863.
Reynolds, Thomas, Westville; died at Nashville, Jan 1, 1863.
Reynolds, John N., Crossing; promoted to Corporal.

Robinson, Robert L., Michigan City; discharged Mar 26, 1863.
Romine, James A., Crossing; mustered out Jul 1, 1865.
Root, Hiram S., Crossing; died near Glasgow, Ky., Nov 5, 1862. Friend of Pvt./Cpl. George Boothe.
Shanly, John, Crossing; deserted Feb 20, 1863.
Shreve, Franklin M., Michigan City; died at Nashville, Dec 9, 1862.
Smith, Andrew J., Michigan City; mustered out. Jul 1, 1865.
Stephens, Justice F. T., Michigan City; killed in action, Stones River, Dec 31, 1862.
Thornton, Samuel, Michigan City; mustered out Jul 1, 1865.
Tuttle, Frederick H., Crossing; died near Nashville, Dec 6, 1862.
Warren, Charles, Crossing; died at Nashville, Mar 4, 1863.
Webster, William W., Westville; discharged Apr 20, 1863.
Webster, Amos G., Westville; promoted to Corporal.
Welch, James, Crossing; transfer VRC Apr 6, 1864.
Williams, Clinton, Westville; mustered out Jul 1, 1865.
Williams, John, Michigan City; deserted Dec 7, 1862.
Williams, John M., Westville; promoted to Sergeant.
Williams, Harrison H., Westville; promoted to Corporal.
Williams, Leander P., Westville; promoted Quartermaster-Sergeant, and on February 13, 1863, to 2nd Lieutenant.

Recruits

Birt, John M., Crossing; mustered out Jul 1, 1865.
Bark, Christian, Manteno, Ill. transfer. to 29th Regt. Jul 1, 1865.
Denham, William, Westville; transfer to 29th Regt. Jul 1, 1865.
Finch, Silas, Westville; mustered out Jul 1, 1865.
Gunter, George N., Valparaiso; died at Nashville, Mar 28, 1864.
McCray, James S., Laporte; transfer to 29th Regt. Jul 1, 1865.
Myers, Charles E., Chicago, Ill.; discharged May 17, 1865.
Spencer, James, Monticello; discharged Feb 12, 1863.
Thornburg, Orlistus W., Westville; transfer to 29th Regt. Jul 1, 1865.
Williams, Charles N., Westville; transfer to 29th Regt. Jul 1, 1865.
Wigmore, James S., South Bend; discharged Nov 4, 1862.
Wilkinson, James B., South Bend; discharged Dec 9, 1862.

Unassigned Recruits

Branson, David A.
Clark, Milo.
Ferrell, Henry
Hatter, Freeborn J.
King, Greenberry
King, Lewis
Miller, William
Miller, William
Rhodes, Michael
Roach, Thomas
Semest, Lewis
Wood, Henry C.

Colonel Gilbert Hathaway

Chapter 16

COLONELS OF THE 73rd INDIANA

Colonel Gilbert Hathaway

Colonel Gilbert Hathaway was born at Sagg Harbor, Long Island, New York, on the 8th day of January, 1813. His father, Gilbert Hathaway, Sr., was a noted shipbuilder who had distinguished himself as the constructor of some of the finest and fastest sailing vessels of that day, and who removed to the city of New York when Gilbert, Jr., was two years old.

At the age of six years the subject of this sketch was placed at school, where he remained until sixteen, and then entered the store of an elder brother as a clerk, where he continued for only one year.

His early ambition was for a liberal education in order that he might choose a profession for himself which should be his vocation for life. But his father, having other plans for the boy, apprenticed him to the carpenter's trade, believing that would be a stepping stone for his ultimate independence.

There being nothing for him to do but obey his father's wishes, he entered upon his duties with that determined spirit that during his whole life was characteristic of the boy and the man.

But he, by no means, lost his desire for an education, to be followed by a profession, and nerving himself to his daily task, he pursued his studies while learning his trade.

The early morning hours found him at his books, and his evenings were spent in the same way. With the assistance and guidance of Bishop Kemper, of the Episcopal Church, he perfected himself in Latin and Greek, and in this laborious manner fitted himself for college.

At the close of his apprenticeship he dropped the implements of his trade and entered Kenyon College, Ohio, in 1833, in his twentieth year, where he was soon distinguished for his scholarship, ranking first in talent of that noted institution.

On leaving college he studied law with the Hon. Henry B. Curtis, of Mount Vernon, Ohio, and was there admitted to the bar.

Soon after his admission to the bar he opened a law office

in La Porte, Indiana, where by his ability and industry he secured a large clientage, and was professionally and socially successful.

At Ogden, New York, in July, 1841, he was married to Sarah Elizabeth Kneeland, daughter of Timothy P. Kneeland, of that city. Their residence was continued at La Porte, Indiana, where five children were born to them, named Annie, Ellen, Curtis Gilbert, Sarah Rose, Elizabeth Lily, and Alfred T. Hathaway.

In his family relations he was very happy, adored by his children and honored by all his dependents.

In July, 1862, he was commissioned by Governor Morton as Commandant of Camp Rose, at South Bend, as a recruiting post for the Ninth Indiana Congressional District, to raise troops to answer the call of President Lincoln in 1862 for 300,000 recruits to assist in crushing the rebellion.

In this camp the Seventy-third and Eighty-seventh Regiments and two companies of cavalry were recruited and mustered into the United States service.

On the 10th of August, 1862, he was commissioned Colonel of the Seventy-third Regiment, which he immediately led to the field, where with but little delay it was ushered into the very front of the war.

In April, 1863, the Seventy-third was chosen as one of the regiments of the "Provisional Brigade" commanded by Colonel A. D. Streight, of the Fifty-first Indiana, to make a raid in the far south. Colonel Hathaway entered into the work of this brigade with all of his well known energy, which was unflagging, until the 2nd of May, during an engagement at Blount's Farm, Ala., he fell mortally wounded while leading his brave men against the foes of his country.

At the end of the war his remains were removed from their place of burial in Alabama and conveyed by a detail from the army, by order of the War Department, to La Porte, where he was buried with appropriate ceremonies in Pine Lake Cemetery, with an escort of the Grand Army of the Republic, Independent Order of Odd Fellows, and a very large concourse of citizens of Northern Indiana. There he rests in the midst of a community "who knew him but to love him."

Lieutenant-Colonel Ivan N. Walker

Lieutenant-Colonel Ivan N. Walker

Ivan N. Walker, son of James and Jane (McBride) Walker, was born February 3rd, 1839, at Arlington, Rush County, Indiana. His parents moved to Fort Wayne, Indiana, where he attended school and grew to manhood.

His first official position was that of Deputy Warden of the Indiana State Prison at Michigan City. He was serving in this capacity when the war began, and in 1862, at the age of twenty-three, entered the service in Company K, Seventy-third Indiana Infantry, and was commissioned Captain of his company August 5th, 1862. He was promoted to Major of the regiment February 13th, 1863. On March 30th, 1863, he was promoted to Lieutenant-Colonel, and resigned July 4th, 1864, on account of disability resulting from long confinement in Libby Prison.

On October 27, 1864, he was married to Miss Anna Layton at Michigan City, Indiana.

He was one of that little band of heroic spirits that escaped by tunneling under the walls of the prison, and he succeeded in eluding pursuit until within sight of the Union camp and flag, when, weakened with sickness and hunger, he was recaptured.

Colonel Walker remained in Nashville after his retirement from the army and served as a Volunteer Aide on the Staff of General George H. Thomas during the siege and battle of Nashville, in December, 1864.

In 1870 he returned to his native state and made his home in Indianapolis, where he served as Deputy County Auditor and State Tax Commissioner for several years, and as a regent of the State Soldiers' and Sailors' Monument until his death..

Colonel Walker's service in the Grand Army was continuous from the date of its organization, and he filled every office in its gift, from Post Commander to Commander-in-Chief, with high fidelity and conspicuous ability.

While serving as Commander of George H. Thomas Post, in 1887, he was appointed Assistant Adjutant-General of the Department by Commander Chase, and was reappointed by the three succeeding Department Commanders. In 1891 he was elected Department Commander, in 1893 Senior Vice-

Commander-in-Chief, and two years later unanimously elected Commander-in-Chief by the National Encampment at Louisville, Kentucky. His last active service was as Assistant Adjutant-General of the Department, to which office he had been appointed for the fifth time.

Colonel Walker was held in high esteem by the National Encampment and always took a prominent part in its deliberations and in shaping its action on important questions.

In his last illness he bore himself bravely and awaited in the confidence and trust that comes to all those who have often listened for the final call in times of great peril and danger, and, when it came, was ready to answer, "Here; Thy will be done," and died, as he had lived, at the post of duty.

In this way he passed from us on the morning of the 22d of September, 1905, in the sixty-seventh year of his age.

"Halt the column, rest a moment,
Let the sounds of battle cease,
An heroic soul is passing,
Passing to the realms of peace."

In beautiful Crown Hill Cemetery, with the flag at half-mast, the impressive burial service of the Grand Army, and the bugle sounding taps, the mortal remains of our comrade were laid to rest.

The family left to mourn his death consists of his widow, Mrs. Anna (Layton) Walker, and his daughters, Mrs. William E. Sharpe and Mrs. Harry D. Hammond, all of whom reside at Indianapolis; and his daughter, Mrs. Charles Caheir, of Paris, France, who has achieved a wide reputation as a vocalist, having appeared in the finest opera houses in Europe.

Colonel Alfred B. Wade

Colonel Alfred B. Wade

Colonel Alfred B. Wade, who began his service with the Seventy-third as Adjutant, was the youngest son of the late Judge Robert Wade. He was born in South Bend, Indiana, December 28, 1839.

His father dying while he was yet quite young, he was reared by his mother with all the care a fond, religious parent could bestow.

His early education was obtained at the old seminary of his native town. When the war broke out he enlisted as a private in the Ninth Indiana Regiment for three months, and was mustered out with his regiment July 29, 1861, at the expiration of term of service.

After joining the Seventy-third Indiana at Lexington, Ky., he continued with it as Adjutant until after the battle of Stone River, when he was promoted to Major, and in that capacity he was with the regiment on the Streight raid, when he was captured and confined in Libby Prison with the other officers.

Through the influence of Hon. Schuyler Colfax, then a member of Congress, his warm personal friend and former Sunday school teacher, he was exchanged in the spring of 1864, and rejoined his regiment at Nashville, Tenn.

He was the ranking officer with the regiment at that time and assumed command, and during the summer of 1864 picketed the Tennessee River between Chattanooga and Decatur.

He was promoted to Lieutenant-Colonel in the latter part of 1864, and was ordered with his regiment to Athens, Ala. After arriving there he began at once to put the fort in better condition for defense and constructed a bomb-proof of his own design which served an excellent purpose.

His command of 500 men was driven into the fort by a rebel force of some 4,000, under General Buford, who demanded his surrender. Colonel Wade refused to surrender and successfully held the fort until Buford withdrew.

He was afterwards commissioned Colonel, but never mustered as such, being mustered out with the regiment as Lieutenant-Colonel in July, 1865.

He kept a diary most of the time during his service, and contemplated writing a history of the regiment, but died before he could find time to prepare it. His diary has been of great use to the committee in compiling this book.

After the war Colonel Wade was married to Miss Jennie Bond, of Niles, Mich. He went with his wife to Ann Arbor, Mich., where he entered the law school of Michigan University. After six months' study he returned to South Bend and entered upon the practice of the law.

He was appointed Postmaster by President Grant, which position he held until his untimely death by accidental drowning in the Kankakee River, while hunting, February 28, 1877.

His services as Postmaster of South Bend gave general satisfaction to the community, and while serving as such he invented an index book which is quite generally used in post offices. His career in civil life was that of a model citizen. He took an active interest in all projects for the advancement of his native state. He was wise in political counsels. His friendships were lasting, and his treatment of enemies was generous. He was an affectionate and loving husband and father, and his loss was one deeply felt, not only by his family, but by the whole community.

Chapter Seventeen

SEVENTY-THIRD INDIANA REGIMENTAL ASSOCIATION

Some five years after the regiment returned home an effort was made to form a regimental association, and a meeting was held on the 8th of September, 1870, at Plymouth, Indiana, at which sixty-one of the comrades were in attendance.

A constitution was adopted, officers elected, and speeches made. Colonel Sumner made the address of welcome, and Colonel Wade made the reply in behalf of the visiting comrades.

General Packard was also in attendance and addressed the meeting, as did Major Calkins, of Rochester. The meeting adjourned to meet at Logansport on December 31, 1871, having elected Captain D. H. Mull president and H. S. Murdock secretary.

This organization, it seems, failed to hold regular meetings and became inactive, but at a reunion of the Soldiers' and Sailors' Association of Northern Indiana and Southern Michigan, held at Valparaiso, October 1, 1885, the Seventy-third men present agreed to meet at Plymouth in August, 1886, with the Ninth and Twenty-ninth Indiana, and hold a joint reunion, and at this meeting a permanent organization was effected, Major William M. Kendall being elected president and Ezra K. Barnhill secretary. A printed journal of that meeting was prepared and issued, and it was entitled, "The First Annual Reunion of the Seventy-third Regiment."

Meetings have since been held annually, and those comrades who have preserved the records of these meetings can, by having the same bound into a volume, have an interesting history of the survivors of the regiment since these reunions began.

At the first annual meeting under this organization in

August, 1886, at Plymouth, Colonel Walker made the address for the regiment, in response to the address of welcome delivered by Hon. H. G. Thayer.

Major William M. Kendall also spoke, and Corporal Justice J. Ferris told how he lost his left arm and all the right hand except the thumb by a murderous shell at Day's Gap, while on the Streight's raid.

The second annual meeting of the Association was held at Logansport, September 21 and 22, 1887, in connection with the Fifty-first Indiana.

Colonel A. D. Streight was present at this meeting, and Captain McConnell made the address of welcome, Colonel Streight and Colonel Walker each making addresses in response thereto. Major Ramsey, of the Fifty-first, Lieutenant Williams, of the Seventy-third, and Captain Wallach, of the Fifty-first, also made addresses.

At this meeting a poem was read from Private Charles H. Doing, of Company K, then living at Bellsville, Md., which was the first of a number of poems contributed by him at these annual meetings. This first contribution was entitled, "Greeting to Comrades," and is as follows:

A grip and a shake of your honest hands,
Old comrades, tried and true,
For we were together in southern lands
In the year of "Sixty-two."

In the grand old days of "Sixty-three,"
And of "Sixty-four" and "Five;"
And I bid good cheer to those who are here,
And the few who are yet alive.

For our ranks, like our locks, are growing thin,
Though our hearts are still warm to each other;
And every brave soldier then mustered in,
I greet as a comrade and brother.

When black iron hail cut gaps in our ranks,
And burnt-powder fog filled the air,
When shoulder to shoulder on Stone River's banks,
We struggled the first to be there.

When comrades lay dying on every height,
And the valleys were strewn with the dead;
When fierce battles raged on our left, on our right,
And the red fires of hell just ahead,

The blood that escaped from our wounds to the ground,
Depleting the fountains of life,
Only strengthened the ties by which we are bound,
For our hearts were made one in that strife.

The third annual meeting was held at South Bend, September 19 and 20, 1888. Mayor Longley made the address of welcome, which was responded to by Major Kendall for the regiment.

At this meeting Secretary Barnhill, who had been denominated the historian of the regiment, made his first report, calling upon members for suggestions, diaries, documents, etc., and for the appointment of committees to aid in the work of compiling and preparing a complete history.

Major Kendall and Lieutenant Williams were appointed a committee to write up a history of prison life, to be added to the regimental history. At the close of the meeting the members all visited Camp Rose and had dress parade again on the old camp ground, a remnant of the Seventy-third band furnishing the music.

After the dress parade Mrs. Colonel Hathaway and Mrs. Colonel Wade were elected honorary members of the Association, both being present and shaking hands with all the comrades.

The fourth annual meeting was held at Chesterton, Ind., September 4 and 5, 1889. Comrade John C. Coulter, of the Forty-eighth Indiana, delivered the address of welcome, which is printed in the record, and was responded to by Major Kendall and Colonel Walker.

Colonel DeMotte, of Valparaiso, also made an address, as did Curtis G. Hathaway, the son of Colonel Hathaway. Curtis G. Hathaway was elected an honorary member.

The fifth annual meeting was held at La Porte, September 3 and 4, 1890. Edward Molloy, of the Eighty- seventh Indiana, delivered the address of welcome, and Sergeant Barnard, of Company K, responded in behalf of the regiment, both addresses being published in the journal.

Curtis G. Hathaway, Colonel Walker, Lieutenant Williams, A. G. Webster, of Company K, and Major Kendall also responded.

The regimental poet, Charles H. Doing, contributed the following poem, which was read by Sergeant Barnard, entitled:

"SERGEANT JONES."

That's old man Jones across the street,
Leaning against the lamp post there,
With tattered-coat and crippled feet,
Bent form and grizzled hair.

Little he looks the hero now,
Such tricks has time played poor old Jones,
With meager locks upon his brow,
And ague-tortured bones.

But eight and twenty years ago,
Responding to the trump of war,
Eager to meet his country's foe,
Went Jones - a very Thor.

Fresh from the headlands of his fields,
Clad in the garb his mother wrought;
Filled with an earnest patriot's zeal,
Victory his only thought.

He was our Color-Bearer then,
And straight as the staff that held the flag,
Always in front, he led the men,
So proud of that "Striped Rag."

Which was his pet name for that banner bright,
By fair hands wrought in Northern homes,
And ever dear to the soldier's sight,
No matter where he roams.

He made a speech when they gave that flag,
A gem in its way, if brevity counts,
A soldier's speech who could not brag,
And whose learning was told by the ounce.

"Ladies," he said, "I take this flag,
And you bet I am proud of the trust."
Then pausing (his words beginning to lag),
"And I'll carry her through, or bust."

For three long years we followed that flag,
Warmed by its presence when blood ran cold,
Through valley and over mountain crag,
Where e'er the war tide rolled.

And when, at the midnight of the strife,
That Christmas week of "Sixty-two,"
Both armies paused, with carnage rife,
As they near Stone River drew.

They paused to test the power of each,
With saber's flash and cannon's roar
To make and fill the deadly breach,
And leaden hail outpour.

There, on that fateful Wednesday morn,
The wiley foe our flank had turned
Surprised our right before the dawn,
A victory brief had earned.

When double-quick we crossed the plain,
To where this bold assault was made,
Our pathway ghastly with the slain,
For dead men filled the glade.

And there, 'mid storm of shot and shell,
Like that on Balaclava's field;
With fire and smoke and "rebel yell,"
The long lines surged and reeled.

There, musket grasped in eager hand,
Waiting for orders to advance,
We lay in line and closely scanned
The battle's wide expanse.

Our men in front, like Spartans sought,
The ground to hold 'gainst fearful odds,
Outnumbered, still, like heroes fought,
And perished there in squads.

O'erpowered at last, reluctant yield,
Close pressed, they stagger through our lines,
Shattered and bleeding from the field,
Like chaff before the winds.

And that dread moment, where was he,
Our Standard-Bearer, staunch and brave?
In front, with his flag, as he swore he'd be,
While flag there was to wave.

The Color-Guards around him lay,
Wounded or dead upon the ground,
Amid the thunder of the fray,
Their lips gave forth no sound.

And still no orders came to rise
We mutely gazed from left to right,
So close the foe we saw their eyes.
With triumph gleaming bright.

Then eagerly our faces turn
To where the colors proudly wave.
The Sergeant's eyes, with purpose burn.
 His thoughts the day to save.

Without command the order gives,
"Uprise !" His voice rings out like a bugle's call,
 "Forward, Seventy-third !" he cries.
"Give 'em a dose of buck and ball !"

At that close range no line could stand
Before that murder-dealing gun,
 As up each sprang at his command.
Four missiles sped as one.

And thus the Hoosiers saved the day,
So much recorded history owns,
And that old wreck across the way,
Is Color-Sergeant Jones."

  The sixth annual meeting was held at Crown Point

September 2 and 3, 1891. Hon. J. W. Youche gave the address of welcome, which was responded to by Lieutenant Williams on behalf of the regiment.

At the camp on the second day Mrs. Colonel Hathaway attended and responded to a call for a speech, in which she expressed her gratification at being able to meet with the members of her husband's old regiment, and spoke of the Colonel having referred with pride, in the daily messages sent home, to his boys of the Seventy-third.

The seventh annual meeting was held at Argos, Indiana, September 7 and 8, 1892, at which Dr. S. W. Gould made the address of welcome, and in the absence of E. A. Jernegan, who had been selected to reply, Sergeant Barnard made the response.

Colonel Walker, Dan H. Hensley, Captain Phelps, and others, also made short addresses. C. H. Doing, the regimental poet, contributed another poem called "The Little Refugee."

The eighth annual meeting was held at Indianapolis, Ind., September 6, 1893, the National Encampment of the G.A.R. being held there also.

At this meeting speeches were made by Comrade Pavey, of the Eightieth Illinois, and A. G. Webster, of Company K.

The ninth meeting was held at Valparaiso, September 5 and 6, 1894. Colonel Suman, of the Ninth Indiana, delivered the address of welcome, which is printed in the Journal, and Colonel Walker responded for the regiment. Colonel Mark L. DeMotte also spoke. C. H. Doing contributed another poem, entitled, "Ike Simmons."

The tenth meeting was held at Lowell, September 4 and 5, 1895, at which Rev. E. P. Bennett made the address of welcome, which was responded to by Lieutenant John G. Greenawalt. Colonel Walker also spoke, as did Hon. Mr. Gregg, of Porter County, and Lieutenant Williams.

The eleventh meeting was held at Westville, September 16 and 17, 1896. The address of welcome was given by Mr. E. T. Scott, and responded to by Lieutenant Williams. An address was also made by Captain Asa Cobb, of the Forty-second Indiana.

The twelfth meeting was held in Michigan City, September 1 and 2, 1897. Mayor Van Dusen welcomed the boys to the city, as also did Rev. P. J. Albright, Chaplain of Rawson Post.

Colonel Walker, in response, made an eloquent address, which was much applauded. Major Kendall, Captain Phelps, Major Williams, and Judge Biddle, of the Eighty-seventh Indiana, also made brief addresses.

The thirteenth meeting was held at Plymouth, September 14 and 15, 1898, when Mayor Jones delivered the address of welcome, which is printed in the Journal, and Colonel Walker and Major Kendall responded thereto for the regiment.

Captain Johnson, of the Ninth Indiana, Major Williams, Comrades Ferris, Gorsuch, Teele, and Herrold, also made brief speeches.

At this meeting the following letter was read from our venerable Chaplain, having been written four days before his death:

"Soldiers' Home, Los Angeles, Cal.
September 5, 1898.
"To the Annual Meeting of the Seventy-third Indiana Regiment:

"My Old Comrades: I am still in the land of the living, but in a bad condition; blind in my right eye, and can see but little out of my left. Away 'long in my eighty-fourth year, and I expect this is the last time I will be able to write to you. Old Comrades, I never forget you. My wish and prayer is that we may all be mustered into the great army above without the loss of one. I am not able to write any more. My love to all the Seventy-third men.

My dear Comrades, farewell.
J. A. FRAZIER,
Late Chaplain Seventy-third Indiana Regiment."

The fourteenth meeting was held on September 20 and 21, 1899, at Logansport. Mayor McKee delivered an address of welcome, which was responded to by Major Kendall and Colonel Walker for the regiment. Major Williams, Captain Swigart, of the Forty-sixth Indiana, and others, made brief speeches.

The fifteenth meeting was held at South Bend, September 5 and 6, 1900, Wilbur E. Gorsuch, President, presiding. This meeting proved to be the largest of any of the annual meetings that have been held, and will not probably be equaled in the future. There were 121 members of the regiment present, besides the honorary members and visitors.

Mayor Schuyler Colfax, son of Schuyler Colfax, who was a member of Congress from that District, and Speaker of the House of Representatives, and Vice-President of the United States afterwards, bade us welcome to South Bend in a brief but eloquent address, to which Judge Barnard responded, both addresses being published in the Journal.

At this meeting addresses were also delivered by Colonel Walker, William Bradford Dickson, Major Williams, and Abraham Lincoln Brick, then member of Congress from South Bend. Judge Barnard read another poem from Charles H. Doing, entitled, "Reunion Poem," and Colonel Walker, Judge Power, of South Bend, John G. Greenawalt, and Judge A. G. Webster all made brief speeches. The poem, and Mr. Brick's address, are published in full in the Journal.

At this meeting Mrs. Wade gave a reception to the members of the Association at her house, where she pinned on each of the survivors a tiny American flag as a souvenir of the occasion. Mrs. Hathaway was also present, and the occasion was one to be long remembered.

The sixteenth annual meeting was held at Chesterton,

September 18 and 19, 1901. There were few in attendance, probably owing to the recent death of President McKinley and the gloom cast by that tragedy over the old soldiers.

Arthur J. Bowser, of the Chesterton Tribune, made an address of welcome, which is published in the Journal, and Major Williams spoke in response for the regiment. John Fuller, the President, presided at this meeting.

The seventeenth meeting was held at New Carlisle, September 17 and 18, 1902. This meeting was of unusual interest, being just forty years after the regiment was at Lexington, and miscellaneous remarks were made by many of the comrades.

Henry H. Deacon, of the One hundred and twenty-eighth Indiana, delivered the address of welcome, and Major Kendall responded.

Major Williams also made a speech and read a poem by Comrade Doing, entitled "A Song of the Camp Fire," which is printed in the Journal.

The eighteenth meeting was held at Crown Point, September 16 and 17, 1903, at which Mr. Frank P. Pattee delivered the welcoming address, which is published in the Journal, and Major Williams responded for the regiment, also reading another poem by Mr. Doing, entitled, "Regimental Poem." This poem is so closely related to the members of the regiment that we will include it in this chapter, as follows:

"REGIMENTAL POEM

When an old-time Union veteran
Hears his regiment will meet
For its annual encampment
To give the boys a treat,

He's apt to think some naughty thoughts,
Of Fortune, if it's so,
He can't be there to meet them,
And figure in the show.

And that's the way this comrade,
In his disappointment feels,
And he growls at fate relentless,
When it frowns at his appeals.

So he must forego the pleasure
Of meeting with them there,
For the state of his exchequer
Won't stand for railroad fare.

But there's not another comrade
In the good old Seventy-third,
Who would enjoy the picnic
As he who sends this word.

Then accept this humble message
As a grace before the fun,
From a distant comrade's heart of hearts;
God bless you, every one.

Aye, faith, 'twould give him pleasure
To meet his comrades there;
For two whole days of leisure,
Their intercourse to share.

To grasp their honest hands,
And greet them as they come;
Oh it makes the old man homesick
To have to stay at home.

Take the regiment by detail,
From A, along to K,
Ten glory shining letters
That gleam like ocean spray.

From the Colonel to the Teamster,
All heroes, staunch and true,
With their colors waving o'er them,
The old Red, White and Blue.

He wants to see Had Williams,
G. Webster and Clark Bales;
He'd rather spend a day with them
Than be the Prince of Wales.

Clate Goodwin and Jut Ferris,
And the boys from Chesterton,
And the journalistic comrade,
His friend, Ed Jernegan.

He wants to hear the rub-a-dub
Of Charlie Pratt's old drum,
As he hammers "Yankee Doodle"
From camp to kingdom come.

He wants to hear Dan Osborn sing,
The songs he used to sing,
And taste, just taste, the apple jack,
John Shanley used to bring.

And a taste would be a plenty,
For if Shanley's ghost could speak,
'Twould tell you that a canteen full
Would kill you for a week.

But the poison had its uses,
And Shanley on its trail,
Would find it though the finding
Brought his shoulder to the rail.

He'd like to try the biscuits
A certain comrade made,
Whose fame for biscuit making,
Of late is much decayed.

Since he's become a poet,
But we've heard it slyly said,
That his biscuits beat his verses,
And they were hard as lead.

Of course, there are some comrades,
Nearer to him than the rest,
Men who shared their blanket with him,
Men with whom he marched and messed.

But they're all as dear as brothers,
Every mother's hero son,
And he begs to be remembered
To each and every one."

    The nineteenth meeting was held at Argos, September 21 and 22, 1904. Dr. Gould delivered the address of welcome, and Major Williams responded for the regiment. Captain James M. Beeber, President, presided at this meeting.
    The twentieth meeting was held at Knox, September 20 and 21, 1905, at which George W. Beeman delivered the welcoming address, and Major Williams made the response.
    The twenty-first meeting was held at Valparaiso, September 19 and 20, 1906, at which Lieutenant Uptigrove, President, presided.
    Mayor Williams delivered the address of welcome, and a response on behalf of the regiment was made by Professor H. B. Brown, with addresses also by Hon. E. D. Crumpacker and Colonel DeMotte, of Valparaiso, and Comrades Caulfield and Herrold.

The twenty-second meeting was held at Westville, September 18 and 19, 1907, John Herrold, President.

E. T. Scott made the address of welcome, responses being made by Professor Brown, of Valparaiso University, Major Williams, A. G. Webster, and Lieutenant Reynolds.

The twenty-third meeting was held at Lowell, September 16 and 17, 1908, Lieutenant Clark, President, presiding.

T. S. Robinson gave the address of welcome, and Major Williams responded for the regiment, and an address was also given by Professor Brown, of Valparaiso, and brief speeches by Comrades Caulfield, Herrold, and others. Major Williams also read another poem by Mr. Doing which we copy in this record, as follows:

"GREETING

If I could be with you, my comrades, to greet you,
And grasp with affection each warm, honest hand,
It would gladden my heart thus kindly to meet you
And prove to you all just how loyal I stand.

I have met some good friends, one time and another,
And I hope to retain them life's rugged march through,
But a war-welded friend is as dear as a brother,
And 'twas there, my old comrades, I mated with you.

How we all marched together, through all kinds of weather,
How foot-sore and weary we tramped to the front; The world may forget it; we're willing to let it,
But while we are living, regret it we won't.

We all did our best for the cause without flinching;
We saw every feature of grim-visaged war;
We stood by our guns when hunger was pinching,
And we followed the flag, like the Wise Men, the Star.

In fancy I see, with unerring precision,
The gathering in of the few who remain,
To taste once again the soldier's Elysian,
With the hope in each heart that we all meet again.

And that's why I'm sorry I can't go to meet you,
And help to rekindle our fast dying fires;
But the bearer, my friend, in my name will greet you,
And say for us both what your meeting requires.

Though .fate, unpropitious, denies me the pleasure
Of joining your revels with story and song;
I'll send you this message, to read at your leisure,
Regretting the author cannot go along.

So good-bye, my friends, let my blessing attend you,
As long as I live I'll be loyal to you;
Though we're most of us grand-dads,
we're still jolly comrades,
And the once lusty rum-lads, who fought the war through."

At this meeting the following letter was received and read from our first Lieutenant-Colonel, Oliver H. P. Bailey:

"Lathrop, Cal.
September 7, 1908.
Comrades: I enclose 50c. U. S. stamps to pay dues. Please do me this kindness. I also request you to extend to the Comrades my best regards. Oh, how much I would like to shake the hand of the best boys that wore the blue - the Seventy-third. I am now 83. I served as a private in the First Indiana in the Mexican War, 1846; as Captain in the Twentieth Indiana, 1861; and Lieutenant-Colonel in the Seventy-third.

With best wishes to you all,
Yours, F.L.C.,
O.H.P. BAILEY."

  The twenty-fourth annual meeting was held at Chesterton, September 15 and 16, 1909, Guy Pratt, President, and Charles A. Pratt, Secretary. The address of welcome was made by J. G. Graessle, and response by the President. Miss Rose Hathaway, daughter of the Colonel, made some interesting remarks.

  These annual meetings have been of great interest to all those who have been in attendance, and the regiment is greatly indebted to Corporal Ezra K. Barnhill for his long and faithful services as secretary, and for his efforts to compile and secure for the regiment a history. He continued in the office of secretary until 1903, when his health failed and he was no longer able to discharge the duties.

  It has been usual for the Association to elect as president someone residing at or near the place of meeting; so while the president was often changed, the office of secretary remained unchanged, until 1903, when H. H. Williams was elected. He served until 1908, when Charles A. Pratt was elected, and he is still in office.

  The objects of the Association are well expressed in the first section of the constitution, as follows:

"The objects of this Association shall be to perpetuate friendships formed in the service during the late War of the Rebellion; to cherish the heroism and memory of our comrades who have fallen in the great struggle; to aid those who have participated with us, their families and dependent ones; and to encourage a love of country and the inseparable Union of the States."

  These objects have been, in the main, faithfully carried out at the annual meetings, by personal intercourse and friendly exercises, in which all the important matters of interest known to each individual in attendance have been recalled and made known to the other comrades.

At the meeting held at LaPorte, in 1890, a paper was read by Sergeant Barnard, giving an account of a visit made the year previous to Huntsville, Triana, Camden, Decatur, and Nashville, in which many facts were recalled of the experiences of Company K, and other companies, while on duty at these various points.

Among the incidents recalled at these annual meetings, which would be of interest sufficient to be preserved in this permanent history, is the incident that occurred on the way from Indianapolis to New Albany, and which resulted in the first death in the regiment, namely, the fact of the men in Company B being knocked off the freight cars while riding on top, and striking against a low bridge. Several of the comrades were injured, but Hannibal Wells, a musician of Company B, was so badly injured that he died at Louisville on the 26th of August, 1862. Many of the boys were on top of the cars at this time, and called in vain to those standing in front of them to look out for the bridge, but they did not hear or comprehend until they were struck.

Many stories have been related of the experiences of the regiment on the march and in camp; some of them recall very plainly the digging in the Cave Hill Cemetery at Louisville, in our effort to fortify the city, soon after our return from Lexington.

Some related to the fact, which is to be regretted, that certain of the men in Companies G and H obtained possession of spurious money, known as "Northern Indiana," which, to some extent, they undertook to circulate, and which acts on their part gave great concern and annoyance to the Colonel, until they were stopped by his orders.

Personal incidents of foraging and hair-breadth escapes have been recited, until it may be difficult for the comrades to tell who was the hero of the incident; and perhaps it does not matter so much, for they are all entitled to have a share in the results.

Some will recall how, at LaVergne, a certain comrade, who had a sense of humor, and whom everyone loved, induced certain recruits to carry up old iron and pile it in front of the Quartermaster's tent, and then to persist in asking him to pay therefore, until the matter became so troublesome that the Quartermaster made complaint to Colonel Wade, and after investigation, he ordered the practical joker to carry the iron away on his own shoulders, as punishment for the joke.

These personal reminiscences are interesting to every survivor, and yet they are but the common inheritance to all volunteer soldiers of the old war, and cannot be distinguished in kind from those so fully collected and published already; and we, for that reason, and because we lack space, will not undertake to gather them up in the story of the Seventy-third Regiment at any great length.

Many such stories are contained in Colonel Hinman's "Story of the Sherman Brigade," and he frequently mentions the Seventy-third, giving many anecdotes known to our boys.

It will be interesting to note that in the report of the Adjutant General of Indiana, published in 1869, appears the following statement relating to battle flags and trophies, which are on deposit in the State Library at Indianapolis, to wit :

"Colors of the Seventy-third Regiment of Infantry. National flag; silk; faded; otherwise in pretty good order; inscribed, 73d Regt. Indiana Vols."

"Regimental flag, blue silk; nearly worn out; inscribed, 73d Regt. Indiana Vols., Chaplin Hills, Ky., Blount's Farm, Stone River, Crooked Creek, Ala., Day's Gap, Ala., Athens, Decatur; rest torn off; staff in pretty good condition."

Some of our comrades, who are reported on the rolls as deserters, were probably captured or lost on our first march from Lexington to Louisville, but in the main it may be assumed that the muster-out rolls, copies of which are included in this history, are correct. The total number of enlisted men when the regiment was formed was 973.

The recruits afterwards received brought the whole

number of the regiment up to 1,169.

This regiment had service a portion of the time in all three branches of the army, the infantry, cavalry, and artillery, if their experience on the Streight raid could be called serving with the cavalry. They perhaps did not wear the yellow stripes that indicated the cavalry, although they were mounted, and performed cavalry duty; yet while at Nashville in charge of the siege guns, a portion of the regiment wore the red stripes as artillerymen.

At the battle of Perryville, Private Swinney, of Company K, was detailed to perform artillery duty, and lost his life on that battle-field.

The memorial resolutions at each annual meeting contain a list, which is fairly accurate, of those who have died each year, and the list of the survivors, which is corrected from time to time, gives a fairly accurate account of those still living, and who are scattered over many states of this Union.

Many of them have reached high places in business, professional, and official life, and afford ample proof of the character of the men who volunteered in the Seventy-third.

Most of them enlisted from purely patriotic motives, because they recognized that their country called them to its defense.

They had no ambition to continue to be soldiers any longer than the necessity existed for their service, and when the confederate army surrendered, and they received their discharges, they at once entered upon the pursuits of peace with alacrity, feeling that their work as soldiers had been well performed, and was ended with the war.

Historical and genealogical notes:

Historical and genealogical notes:

Historical and genealogical notes:

www.ingramcontent.com/pod-product-compliance
Lightning Source LLC
Chambersburg PA
CBHW031313150426
43191CB00005B/205